THE PAINTER'S KEYS
A SEMINAR WITH ROBERT GENN

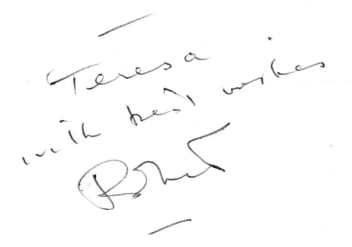

Teresa
with best wishes
Robert

THE PAINTER'S KEYS
A SEMINAR WITH ROBERT GENN

Copyright © 2003 by Robert Genn
Studio Beckett Publications
12711 Beckett Road
Surrey, B.C.
Canada
V4A 2W9

Second Printing 2003

Canadian Cataloguing in Publication Data

Genn, Robert, 1936-
  The painter's keys

  Includes bibliographical references and index.
  ISBN 1-55056-479-X

  1. Art – Vocational guidance I. Title.
N8350.G46 1996   702'3   C96-910798-6

Printed and bound in Canada by
Friesens Corporation
Surrey, B.C.

ALSO BY ROBERT GENN

In Praise of Painting

The Dreamway

Editor's Preface

Robert Genn is a walking encyclopaedia of information, quotations, anecdotes, stories, and opinions. He is also an artist of international stature and brilliant success. His seminar, 'Professionals' Guide,' has been given in various forms over the past several years. The text of this book has been largely taken from a two day seminar held in the Centennial Room of the Memorial Arena in Kelowna, British Columbia, Canada. The Kelowna School of the Arts under the direction of Donovan Harrison was the sponsor. The 39 participants were all artists, except for one artist's agent. There were 22 women and 17 men ranging in age from teens to elderly.

Most of the items and exchanges have been edited for clarity and brevity. Certain problems are encountered in adapting seminar proceedings to book format, not the least of which is the wandering nature of spoken thought. To help in the logical accessing of the material we added an 'idea index' at the end of the book. The 'key words' and other information handed out by Mr Genn are included in an appendix.

The seminar was made up of ten sessions of almost one hour each, and these sessions form the ten chapters of the book. In a few cases additional material from later seminars has been added.

The participants are identified only as *(Man)* and *(Woman)*. It was not possible to accurately identify all of the speakers, and it was rationalized that they spoke for all artists. The editor offers apologies for the occasions where brilliancy or insight goes unattributed. It would also have been useful for the reader to know the approximate age of the participants, but it was decided to leave this out. Sexism seemed enough.

There was a lot of laughter, and some gasping and applause from time to time in this seminar. The notation: *(laughter)* and other activities were recorded in the first draft. It seemed to add animation to the material. But after some consideration the laugh-track was left out.

A few personal and localized items, while often amusing or locally informative, have been removed from the text. Sometimes the group became distracted. At one point Alice Duck came forward and read Robert's runes. This sort of material has also been left out.

Robert's system is to keep pushing ahead with his ideas and the needs of the participants – and they all seemed to vigorously keep going until they ran out of time. It is remarkable how essential and valuable these ten hours turned out to be.

Peter Gellatly,
Editor
February 28, 1997

Introduction

The idea in these encounters is for participants to glean as much information from each other and from the group leader as is possible in the allotted time. I try to guide the group to what I think they need to know without doing a workshop job of demonstrating how I think they should draw and paint – even though the subject of technique creeps in from time to time. Anyone who has an idea, or a thought, or a question, is encouraged to just blurt it out. My reasoning is that if they are ready for it, we should all be ready for it. While I have an agenda I try to be casual and not worry about getting all my stuff in order. If we get waylaid by taxation, or something equally mundane, I just let it happen – I accept what people want to hear about. If we become distracted I try to sense whether the group wants to deal with it, and I steer accordingly.

I have found from these seminars that artists frequently pick up one or two or three things that improve their performance and the way they approach their jobs. From the letters I receive I know many participants have become more fulfilled as artists, some are even outrageously successful. The idea is to become a more effective artist. We are all looking for systems that will help us re-motivate or re-assess, or to become more creative. If I do my job right everyone stays alert and open-minded. An advertisment for the seminar says: "Each participant will take away an enriched understanding of where he or she is going with new and regenerated confidence with which to make it happen."

Participants are given some printed material and a bibliography to be referred to in the proceedings. I ask everyone to cruise through the key words at their leisure – a system that seems to trigger thoughts, ideas, and concerns for people like us. I encourage the adding of their own key words, and invite them to talk about them if they wish. From time to time in the seminar I mention the sources and the stimulus for my ideas as well as references to fertile areas they may not know about. (See the appendix and bibliography at end of the book.)

The Kelowna seminar was fairly typical of the sort of groups I see. There were eight individuals who claimed to be professional artists – making a living from their art.

Ten said they considered themselves on the borderline between amateurism and professionalism – still working at another job, but about to make it soon. One said she was a retired artist, one an artist's manager.

Nine said they worked primarily in oil, twelve in acrylic, fourteen in watercolor, two in other media. Fifteen said they worked in more than one medium.

Five were art students from the local college. Four were commercial artists. Two said they were "commercial-artist-fine-art-wannabees." Several said they were "conceptual"; there were several "realists," and several "impressionists." One was "just thinking about being an artist." Two were published writers.

One woman considered herself a professional artist but wasn't making a living at it, and told me she thought my definition of "professional" was too narrow.

I would like to thank those persons who have helped me in my thinking during the last couple of years, and those who checked and advised me on this material: Sheila Ablitt, Robert Bateman, Judi Betts, Robbie Dunfield, Kerry Erickson, Peter Ewart, Andree Fleming, Tom Fleming, Dorothy Gale, Jennifer Garrant, David, James and Sara Genn, the late and sadly missed Jack Hambleton, Donovan Harrison, Gisela Harrison, Don Hutchinson, Cathryn Jenkins, Leila Kaiser, Brian Knowles, Craig McLachlan, David MacLagan, Robert McMurray, Richard Nelson, Toni Onley, Lance Peverley, Joe Plaskett, Ellen Poole, Deborah Putman, Grame Shaw, Dr Peter Steel, Mike Svob, Arla J. Swift, Lana Underhill, Linda Wagner, Glennis Zilm and others of the artistic brotherhood and sisterhood.

Special thanks go to Peter Gellatly, senior editor of the Haworth Press of New York, who cleaned up the manuscript while saving some of the energy of the occasion and the personalities of the participants.

Those who took part in the Kelowna Seminar were: Alice Anderson, Audrey Anderson, Allen Arndt, Jim Barr, Helen Beattie, Gordon Derbyshire, Alice Duck, Sheldon Gray, Terry Greenbrough,

Bob Harold, Rosalyn Haynes-Norman, Burton Hennig, Fay Hilker, Liz Hodgkinson, Betty Howe, Noreen Jodoin, Bill Jurome, Lee Koffski, Doris Lambert, Gary Langrish, Dr Joe Leicester, Jack Messett, Dennis Nielson, Linda Nardalli, Colleen Owens, Vic Pauls, Alice Pearson, Rosalind Robertson, Murray Roed, Rita Routley, Mary Savoy, Eileen Sawracki, Marie Scott, Muriel Skae, Tom Steiner, Emily Taylor, Kerin Toth, Barbara Wright, and Kyle Yakimovitch. To these and all the other creative people that I have met during encounters of this sort, I would like to say thank you for your wisdom, your sharing, and for helping me to bring form to some of my ideas.

A wonderful variety of people attend seminars. It would be easy to simply call them 'artists,' which they all are, and be done with it. In reality some participants are youthful and idealistic, while others are elderly and idealistic. Still others are honed by decades of practicalities, and their concerns reflect this. These days there are many young artists who crave definitive answers to specific questions. When seminars begin, and I look out at the shining faces, I realize the responsibilities we all bear for one another. When seminars end, my hope is that I haven't passed on too much foolishness.

Robert Genn,

Vancouver, B. C.

March 5, 1997

Contents.

"Somewhere over the rainbow, bluebirds fly ...
Why, then, oh why can't I?"

E.Y. Harburg

Hour 1

The Child and the Recipes

(Genn)   One day when I was a toddling child I was down by the hollyhocks in our garden and I found a mole. I turned it over and looked at its marvelous little face and discovered its tiny hands. I'd never seen a mole before, or even knew one had hands, and I was flooded with a feeling of joy.

Something I am going to try to bring to you in this seminar is that as adults we should learn to daily and hourly dig out our wondering child and train ourselves to always look at what we are seeing as if it were "baby-eyes" new. When we develop again this way of seeing, our life and our work becomes fresher. We don't repeat ourselves so readily, and we don't become jaded. As I have explored my possibilities as a visual artist I found that this attitude became central to my happiness.

I've played and experimented with other systems, like self-organization, and watching the clock, and meeting deadlines – but I wanted a mode of productivity that was so natural and so joyous that good work came along automatically. I remembered the little mole I had found when I was a child and it gave me the key. It was elusive and difficult to achieve at first, but I was able to find it – for the minutes and hours of my workdays.

I call it 'The Joy Mode'. When you have this mode working for you, you will produce automatically, your quality will improve, and things will happen for you, and you will have what appears to be good luck. I searched for a long time before I found what this 'Joy Mode' is, and I want to try to describe it for you.

A wonderful British potter, the late Michael Cardew, spent a great deal of his life trying to understand creative joy. He said: "If you are lucky, and if you live long enough, and if you trust your materials and you trust your instincts, you will see things of beauty growing up in front of you, without you having anything to do with it."

He suggested you have to be a bit lucky, and you've got to spend some time at it. Then you must trust your materials, that is, you are on intimate terms with the media of your choice; paints, brushes, supports. You should be on a first name basis with your materials. And most importantly you learn to trust your instincts. You get up in the morning and say, "This job is right for me today", and you know it. You're not being influenced by outside forces, or by guilt or obligation.

With Michael Cardew's insight I changed my daily routine. I sort of became born again. I had flirted with this concept many times in my creative life, and one day I fell head over heels for it. I began to look at my work as new and was more encouraged to continue with it. Somehow, after a few minutes, a little bird told me what was going to give joy. It might be a big or small project, a challenge or an easy piece. I was propelled to the easel, squeezing paints with joy. The work flowed and was buoyant and showed confidence – sometimes it was even – dare I say it – good work.

"You will see things of beauty growing up in front of you, without you having anything to do with it." And when those things of beauty are not as beautiful as you had hoped – that is part of the game too. Your failures can be joyful, because they are the stepping-stones to your successes.

Here's another way of looking at this idea. Mihaly Csikszentmihalyi has researched and popularized a concept which he calls "Flow." He looks for the optimization of experiences in all areas of life. If we are prepared to accept happiness as a worthwhile goal, we gain "flow" by a total involvement in the chosen activity, through concentration and the recognition and appreciation of complexity. With three essential components: craft, *con brio* and connection, we reach what musicians call 'performance level,' which heightens the satisfaction, improves the success rate, and minimizes failure.

Craft means building your skills and techniques to high levels of excellence.

Con brio means working – performing – with elan, brilliancy, dash. You are a *maestro,* a master.

Connection means lacing your work with meaning for others.

(Man) You mentioned failures. We all have lots of them. Should failures be reworked or discarded?

(Genn) Weak artists cling to their failures, keep them around, and live with the dream that they can some day be made to fly. Strong artists who are in a mood to grow gather them up and burn them. Burning is one of the most satisfying and releasing creative acts. Get rid of the ones you don't like. You are in the joy mode and you have the intuition and the courage to say "I know I don't like it." The opinions of others are not important. You'll gain strength by getting rid of the things you don't like. As sculptress Cathryn Jenkins says: "Put the chisel in the crack and give it a good whack."

(Man) I heard someone say to re-paint your paintings, seven, eight times and that seems to have some value for me. I seem to learn.

(Genn) If you have the spirit to break out a new canvas and tackle an old subject, then do it.

(Man) I re-do recent failures. Not old ones.

(Genn) There is value in that. Some people have the metabolism to do it, but I'd say most of us lose interest and the creative enthusiasm in a subject and we would rather turn to another. You may be one of the artists who can handle that kind of re-working. You should do what suits you best. However, if you leave unsatisfactory paintings around your studio, you may repeat your own mistakes. Poor paintings can jinx your muse and delay your natural growth.

(Woman) Are you saying that you completely gesso it over?

(Man) Yes, start again. Learn from what you've done and carry on.

(Woman) I have a lot of paintings that I like, probably about two hundred, but they haven't sold. I don't think burning them would be the answer. They're in the way.

(Genn) Mentally in your way?

(Woman) Yes, there is something stopping me from going ahead. What should I do with them? Have a sale, give them away?

(Genn)   Here are a couple of suggestions. I didn't have the courage to burn some things that were borderline, so I built another studio at the bottom of my property. I call it my *'salon des refusees.'* It's a low-tech studio, there is no telephone, no radio, only an old pot-bellied stove. This is where I store my problematical paintings – the unburnables– in a sort of limbo. I have the same volume of paintings as you, but every once in a while I feel like having a day with these old acquaintances and I go down to that studio and play around. Sometimes I rework them. Sometimes I reline them.

(Woman)   What do you mean by reline?

(Genn)   I cut the canvas from the stretcher and glue it with different cropping to a new support of either wood or canvas.

(Woman)   In answer to the lady who has too many paintings around I suggest she take them somewhere and have them critiqued. She needs an objective opinion, someone who will weed out the good from the bad.

(Genn)   You should be your own best critic and have the courage to do your own weeding. You are hoping that some authority will say, "This is good, and this is bad, and this should go directly to the Guggenheim." Rugged individualists are fully in charge of their own quality control. Beginning artists, beginning writers, anybody who is taking a chance tends to hang their ego on their efforts, hoping – just hoping – that the quality is there. Early dross should be eliminated so that we can grow beyond. I call this seminar "Professionals' Guide." It invites you to become a professional. Professionals put their amateur thinking behind them.

(Woman)   Is it unprofessional to sell your older work when it is not in line with something you are doing right now?

(Genn)   If you are worried about the continuity of your image – don't bother. If collectors want your early work, let them have it – but only if you can live with it yourself. And take heart in the knowledge that for every person who likes your early work there is someone who loves your new.

(Man)   Not to belabor the point, but this is a problem with me. I have often at a weak moment given paintings to family members, my wife in particular, and later on I don't like the painting and

it hangs in my home and I have to live with it. My wife won't give it up, what do I do? Do I engineer a burglary?

(Genn)   Offer to trade for work you consider superior. I try to make sure that the paintings I give away to friends and loved-ones are the very best I can do. People with less developed taste or less fussy standards will always find something they like in your studio, especially if it's free. Try to steer them in the right direction.

(Man)   I'd like to comment about selling older paintings. I have painted for eighteen years, and I don't think that, just because a painting is old, means that it is a bad painting. I believe that over the course of time there is one painting meant for everybody – and if it takes five years for that certain person to come along and select that older painting, then so be it.

(Genn)   There is a collector for every painting above a certain level, the rest should be incinerated.

We can all tell stories of paintings that stayed around for a long time. I had one of a Dalmatian dog jumping up on a girl in a spotted dress. It was a happy painting, well painted, and fresh looking. It had been to at least a dozen galleries at one time or another and I discovered it again in my 'salon des refusees'. I pulled it out and loved the spots all over again, so I sent it off to a gallery that hadn't had it before. Right away a discriminating connoisseur wandered in and bought it. I think he had his own Dalmatian and a daughter with a spotted dress.

There is somebody for every painting – even your poor ones. The point is do you want the poor ones to be out and around in the world?

(Woman)   How do you feel about putting the date on paintings?

(Genn)   About fifteen years ago I stopped dating paintings; they stay fresher that way. When a dealer or a collector turns over a painting and sees an older date on it they sometimes think there must be something wrong with the painting. I should add that many collectors like to know the date of a painting, and for these people I make it possible for them to find out.

(Woman)   How?

(Genn)   I make the date, location, and other information available to the buyer on enquiry.

(Woman)   Authors often don't sell their writing easily, but we assume that paintings are supposed to just go out the door.

(Man)   I've never supposed that.

(Genn)   If a dealer is exhibiting your work, and people are seeing it, it is doing the best it can. If you would have your paintings on other peoples' walls you should ask yourself, "What business am I in?" I think you should be in the business of communicating feelings, and if you are not doing that, all this shifting and moving stuff around isn't going to make a great deal of difference. E.M. Forster said: "Only connect." He was talking about our job as artists. His idea was to concentrate on the transfer of a valuable feeling to another person. When you have your wondering child and the joy mode going for you – that is the first step toward making a connection.

(Woman)   I've tried being joyous and childlike, but I'm afraid my work is still only – childlike.

(Genn)   That childlike part of your work is an important step for you. I hope to show that the wondering child is only a part, and a prerequisite, for the greater trip.

(Woman)   I'm constantly disappointed and frustrated on that trip.

(Genn)   I think it's more like a yellow brick road. There is a surprise around every corner; some parts are beautiful, some perverse; along the way you meet friends who have similar problems. Devilish witches await you. You discover that it is more difficult to get to Oz than you originally thought.

I'd like now to draw your attention to another way of thinking – a recipe way of thinking. This, you might say, is a more grown up way of approaching your job.

A few years ago I did a demonstration for a group of artists and I took a friend with me who was not an artist. He sat quietly at the back of the room with his arms folded, watching what I did, listening to the questions. On the way home he said, "They are all looking for the secret, and the secret is that there is no secret." I had to tell him that there are secrets, and that they can and are picked up from other artists, and that artists can claim the secrets for themselves.

I recommend making up lists – or recipes if you like. In the heat of the job it is easy to forget the richness that you might bring to your work. Sergi Eisenstein, the great Russian film-maker, was asked about his method of directing, and he said, "Careful planning, and brilliant improvisation." When you go out with a script, you have an advantage.

Your lists should be your own personal lists. They would be of systems you use: plans, directions, techniques. They can be simple and obvious, or they can stretch your highest capabilities. Our seminar today and tomorrow is not a workshop on how to paint, but I want to give you a sample list such as you might make up yourselves. These are items that I currently think about when I'm painting, and I try to improvise on them as brilliantly as I can. You will have your own list. That's what makes your work unique. You name the ideas – and you claim the ideas. They become yours because you have thought them through.

Robert Henri, who wrote the wonderful book called *The Art Spirit*, said, "There is no art without contemplation." When you come to an area in a painting you have the knowledge that you have thought about it before – your brush does not just wander aimlessly. You know how unsatisfactory it is to be in the middle of a work and have the feeling that you don't know what the dickens you're doing. You are in a mess. Whereas, when you use 'name it and claim it,' you can say to yourself, you are in the 'reflected light' area of the work, or you are in the 'warm against cool.' It seems so simple and obvious, but it is valuable. Let me go through this list and explain what I think when I see my own notes. Think about these as little recipes.

Equal intensity lay-bys: Colours of the same intensity and brightness are laid side by side so they vibrate with one another, creating excitement.

Defocus: Paintings that are equally sharp and focused are boring. When we work from life, our eyes dart around the subject, focusing on each item, and this creates a problem. Real life is different. When each of you look at me I am in focus, but the no-smoking sign up here beside me is not. Your paintings will pick up life if subjects you wish to feature are sharper, and secondary elements softer.

The big blur: Blur some subjects and areas in your paintings.

Create mystery and paucity. Paucity means smallness of number or quantity. In art it means the minimal expression needed to convey the form or idea.

Warm against cool: Place warm (red, orange, yellow) colours adjacent to cool (purple, blue, green) to give visual interest.

Adjacent areas accepting temperature: Charles Reid, in *Painting What You Want to See* shows how you can achieve harmony in your work by including the colour of an object in its surroundings and so relating the parts to the whole.

Reflected light: Many artists don't know anything about reflected light. I think they never noticed it, or, with their jaded adult eyes, resisted seeing it. Reflected light enhances quality and makes subjects live. To give you an example of reflected light, there is a lady here with a purple-pink sweater, and the colour glows on the underside of her chin.

Contrapuntal over-emphasis: This is where you give counterpoint to your main theme by emphasizing secondary elements. Draw attention to normally uninteresting areas through care of design.

Reinforcement of negative areas: Try to see your work in terms of negative areas – featuring the patterns between elements of the painting. Fit the sky down into the trees. Pop in the lights or darks behind the wicker chair.

Held and lost edges: Make elements in the work soft and then hard; make lines come and go. Evaporate some things and let the viewer's eye behold some mystery and excitement.

Gradations: Great paintings have gradations, large and small. Fit them around one another. They serve to lift the subject off the two-dimensionality of the canvas. Gradations are an essential abstract convention. As watercolourist Judi Betts says; "Don't go two inches without changing the color or the tone."

Colour surprise: These are the heightened points of colour in your painting that bring it to life. In order to make colour surprise work you must have an absence of strong colour in other areas. The hunter in the sombre landscape wears a red jacket.

Coming to light: To come to light, move up the colour wheel (in other words toward twelve o'clock – yellow) and add white. Conversely, to come to shadow, move down the wheel and add black. For example, to give the sunny side of orange, move up to yellow orange, and add a little white.

Activation: These are spots of colour or pattern that circulate around in the painting, controlling and leading the eye of the viewer.

Strong value composition: Great paintings have great patterns. A checkerboard or a contrasty tiled floor are satisfying to the eye. Victor Vasarelli, and others, explored and expanded on this idea.

Inter-patterning: See the elements of the painting as patterns, and work them together. For example, make tall and enfolding grass turn into the striped dress of a young lady.

Local colour conceptualizing: This means allowing a chosen colour in a painting to become the mother-colour to all the other colours. A painting which features a bright red sweater as a center of interest might lean toward red in other areas.

The real see: The Canadian painter A. Y. Jackson noted that 'failure of sight' was a tiresome problem. He meant we should be able to look at our work-in-progress as if it were previously unseen. He suggested laying the painting aside. Working on several paintings at the same time facilitates this. The idea is to surprise yourself by catching the painting out of the corner of your eye, or in a mirror, or in another room. Catch it, and size it up.

The joyous stroke: More than any other element in your work, your brush stroke tells about your personality and your caring. It's your signature. Take a good look at your strokes and see who you are – fresh, fiddly, elegant, constipated, grand.

Talk back: Let your painting talk back to you. Clear your mind by looking out the window for a few moments. Then, as honestly as you are able, let the painting tell you what it needs. You are not forcing it to have what your mind tells you it should have, but rather what it now needs. It's a different way of thinking.

Flats: Some areas on a painting can be painted flatly, without gradation or variation, often with a strong local colour. Over-rule the tendency to imitate unimportant minor nuances in nature such as the details of lawns or sand. Keep some areas simple.

Tie-ins: Areas that come to one another and blend into one another. For example, from where you are seated, my sweater is nearly the same colour as the blackboard, and could be rendered as one unit. Your mind tells you that there is a line running down my shoulder, but you don't need to put in what your mind tells you.

Pink focus: Emphasize a pink nose, pink elbows, knees, or fingers. This is a small convention which gives life and energy to figure work.

Avoidance of knowns: Knowns are boring. Try to find the surprising alternates. Avoid the obvious cliche. Inflict your own unique flavor and personality on the work.

This is an incomplete and serendipitous list. Did you notice that some items are contradictory? In creativity, contradiction is a principle. Also, some concepts are very close to one another – but they have subtle differences. This is where decision and choice and taste are called upon. My object in presenting this list is to help you to ask yourself what you want to have in your list.

(Woman)   You mentioned Robert Henri and Charles Reid. Could you comment on them?

(Genn)   Robert Henri is best known to most of us as the author of *The Art Spirit*. He was a great American artist and teacher. His death in 1929 brought to an end a life of uncontaminated devotion to art. He had a wide influence with artists in the days when quality was still taught in schools. He had innovative ideas. One of them was that his students should work in one room with the model set up in another, so the students would have to go back and forth with the information in their heads.

The other book that I mentioned was *Painting What You Want To See*, by Charles Reid. Reid paints exceptionally well in both oils and watercolour. This book, and others by him, are illustrated with his and his students' work. You look at those illustrations and then try to determine what is on his mind and what he is going to say about them – and very often he surprises you. His comments challenge the way you previously looked at things, and build the range of your capabilities.

(Man)   How important do you think creativity is?

(Genn)   Claude Levi-Straus had a theory that there is no such thing as individual creativity. He suggested that we "never create absolutely, we only choose certain combinations from a repertoire of ideas which it is possible to reconstitute." This is bad news for artists who are always pulling rabbits out of hats and getting credit for opening new vistas. However, for anyone who attends the great art show-places of the world, it comes as no surprise to find that similar works appear everywhere with different signatures. The collective consciousness, according to Levi-Straus, is like a big pot of lentil soup from which we all ladle into our personal bowls. We have to ask ourselves a few questions here. Would it be unreasonable for artists to simply act as if they were being original with every creation? If the ladling produces something that is new to the beholder – is it new? How valuable is the concept of "new"?

What I call creation often sneaks up and surprises me when I am in the act of repetition. Sir Lawrence Olivier said it was better to repeat a line ten times than to talk for two days on how it would best be delivered. With repetition, the alternate approaches become clear, the options open. This is professional creativity.

(Woman)   I disagree. The opposite is true. By not repeating something, the door is opened to new experiences and new avenues. If producing new ideas for creativity doesn't work, why are we going to talk here for two days?

(Genn)   Is talk creativity?

(Woman)   The purpose of seminars is to ingest a volume of new perspectives, and to claim the ideas for which individuals have an affinity. Seminars are part of contemplation. It is up to the individual to use his own means to put the ideas he has contemplated to work so that the artist can grow and develop and improve.

(Genn)   Peter Ewart, one of Canada's senior artists, likes to compare the life of an artist to the assault on a great mountain such as Everest. Hundreds start from the valley, but only a few make it to the top. Some stay mired in the gumbo and the devil's-club, but they too contribute to the climb. In Peter's words, "They climb the Lotze Face and then they may reach the South Col. Some may camp for what seems to be a lifetime on the Col." According to Peter

Ewart, no matter how far the individual climbs they should be satisfied just to be included on the great mountain.

Artists have an obligation to do their personal best. It's a commitment to the child in you – and to the adult capabilities of gathering those things that you need to fine-tune your craft. Put the two together and you will have an almost religious conviction – a passion for your work.

Here's a little statement of feeling – perhaps it's a sort of artist's prayer:

"The world's engagement of beauty is my bible,
and Art is my religion.
I come to it as a child,
and I add all the grown wisdom I can gather.
Creativity is my salvation.
My easel is the altar.
My paints are the sacraments.
My brush is my soul's movement,
and to do poorly, or not to work, is a sin."

Hour 2

The Better Artist

(Genn)   In every bad artist there is a better artist trying to come out. I start with the proposition that we all have, within ourselves, the potential and the qualities needed to excel.

A couple of years ago I did a demonstration painting in front of two groups of grade-school children. There were grade four children, who sat on the floor in front of me, and grade eight children, who sat in desks behind. It was a two part session. After I had completed a small painting they were asked to go to their own rooms and paint something that was based on what they saw me do. During my demo the children were very quiet and followed my progress with attention, and when I finished I asked them for questions. Most of the questions came from the younger children. The older ones remained cool and reserved, perhaps because they didn't want to show their ignorance or to appear too interested. I think some of them even regarded me with some suspicion.

Then they went to their respective rooms and painted for an hour, while I went around and looked at their paintings. The small children did a rather better job than the older children. They produced big fresh paintings with bright colours, and the subject matter ran right out to the edges. Their paintings were loaded with creative joy. Most of the older children did fiddly little pictures in the middle of the canvas – they were generally correct in proportion, well enough drawn, and they were all unfinished when the bell rang. The younger children had most of their painting done while the older ones were just getting going. From this and other experiences like it I have been able to draw some conclusions.

My feeling is that if we are to be effective artists we should learn to extract the young child that is within us all. It's the child that makes the artist. In my reading I found that some psychologists believe that it's the child in us that is the source of all our joy, indeed, it's the facility that has us fall in love. It would seem that unless we get the child working within us we are at a serious disadvantage.

Furthermore, it has been my observation that artists of the right brain persuasion have less trouble accessing their child. Recent findings have indicated that successful creativity depends on the interplay of both hemispheres of the brain and the ability to easily transpose hemispheres.

(Woman)   How do you know if you are left or right?

(Genn)   By how you think. Right brainers tend to make unusual connections out of commonplaces. Right brain thinking made it possible for Picasso to combine bicycle handlebars with a bicycle seat into the horned head of a mysterious and threatening animal.

There are several ways of testing yourself to see which hemisphere is dominant. Here is a quick test that I find useful, but it is by no means definitive: Note which eye you automatically use when you look through the viewfinder of your camera. If you tend to use your left eye you are probably right-brained. The characteristic does not necessarily have anything to with left-handedness and right-handedness.

Popular education is slanted towards the higher percentage of the population which tends to be left-brained.

It has been said that this is why our society turns out so many accountants and lawyers. Probably, though, a high percentage of people in this seminar will be right-brained, and, ironically, many of you will be married to left-brainers.

The understanding of bicameralism is not new. Lao Tsu, the Chinese philosopher who has been dead now for 2500 years, developed concepts of intuition and the balancing of yin and yang for the progress of creativity and self-realization.

Right-brainers have a capicity to see things in a holistic and general way. They size up patterns and designs faster and with more facility. They see the forest when others see the trees. But as our education, our way of life, and the expectations of society tend to force us into the left-brained mode, our job is to go back and access our true nature. I don't believe Emily Carr, for example, discovered the child that was within her until she was in her late fifties. Up to that time her work was of average interest and quality. Then about 1930, she started painting in what she called "the marvelous modern manner." Her work went grand, personal, sweeping, and free.

A book you may find useful is *How Creative are You?* by Eugene Raudsepp. It contains a series of tests. You will find your scores fascinating, especially when you compare them with the scores of your associates.

(Woman) I have a husband who is very direct and systematic and goes from this to this to this; he drives me crazy and I drive him crazy.

(Genn) And of course the way he goes about his life is just as valid as the way you do.

(Woman) I know that, but he doesn't.

(Genn) If you want to pursue some of these ideas further there is an excellent book called *Art, Mind and Brain,* by Howard Gardner. It is loaded with the findings of child psychologists, and those who have been interested in creativity from a psychological and physiological point of view. In this book you will meet an autistic child by the name of Nadia, who, at the age of three was producing the most marvelous drawings. There seemed to be a relationship between her inability to speak and the way she expressed herself through art. Later, when she entered a group home and began to relate to other children and learn basic verbal skills, her art appeared to decline. All autistic children do not of course become great artists. It is important not to jump to conclusions, but it seems possible that the development of language hampers creativity.

There is some evidence for this idea. Take, for example, the concept of 'the red barn.' This is a literary idea and a linguistic cliche, although it conjures up a picture. I've noticed that older, verbally skilled artists tend to paint the barn red, even though the one they are looking at might be a sort of washed-out rust colour, or even grey. They are not seeing the barn, but hearing what their brain knows about barns.

The presence of this condition promotes all sorts of interesting ideas. Say you had an art school where neither the students nor the instructors were allowed to speak. A vow of silence like that in a monastery would prevail. My guess is that facility and creativity would flourish with a speed not previously seen.

(Man) I think it's important to forget all the rules. Sometimes I do a good painting if I forget the rules and just let my feelings flow.

(Woman) Like the grade eights at your demo, we are sometimes concerned with what is expected of us, and that holds us back.

(Genn) Yes, we have a feeling of obligation and perhaps guilt. Education and parental influence have taken their toll. Furthermore, the grade eight students tend to be highly influenced by their peers. By the time they are in their teens many young people have become rugged conformists.

(Man) Your argument is that we must return to a childlike attitude. But this runs counter to maturing and bringing our adult mind to bear. Problems are not simple. Our culture teaches us to grow up.

(Genn) That's correct. The idea of accessing your child is essentially anti-social. If you do it, you will be bucking the system. Even the Bible tells us in Corinthians; 'When I was a child, I spoke as a child, I understood as a child, but when I became a man, I put away childish things.'

(Man) I think working quickly and not belaboring, makes my work better.

(Genn) Yes. A doctor can have four appendices out before breakfast. That's professionalism. If you or I had to take out an appendix, we would go by the book, take until noon, probably lift the wrong organ, and the patient would likely not make it to the recovery room. That's amateurism.

(Man) I love to draw. Drawing gets me going.

(Genn) Drawing is still the bottom line. A day or two after Michaelangelo passed away, someone found in his studio a piece of paper on which he had written a note to his apprentice: "Draw, Antonio, draw, Antonio, draw and do not waste time."

(Woman) Youth has less experience with failure. An older person fears failure because he has had more of them.

(Woman) What about using music in the studio to get the better artist out of ourselves?

(Genn) It has been shown that baroque music; Mozart, Vivaldi, Bach, etc., opens the floodgates of creativity. It seems to me that music provides a mantra, which occupies a portion of the brain and frees the other portion to create. The hum of an automobile engine does very much the same thing. You may have noticed that creative thoughts come easily when you are at the wheel. In music, the regularity, the beat and the repetition, which are particularly evident in baroque music, sets the brain into the right mode.

(Woman) I use 'new age' music.

(Woman) I use baroque music for creating and for studying. I find rock and romantic music are counterproductive.

(Genn) Perhaps the lyrics, when you think about them, throw you off track. The idea seems to be to fill a part of your mind with music that has an abstract quality.

(Man) I once heard the remark that "self-consciousness is the enemy of art."

(Genn) How do you interpret that?

(Man) Just let it flow without influence of brain or ego.

(Woman) I tried to think about what I did as a child. I used to love running – and so when I go into my studio in the morning I do spot-running to music. I find this frees up my creativity. The energy starts to move in my body, and I'm ready to be a child at the canvas.

(Genn) Jogging 'jogs' creativity.

(Man) I think it is a good idea to paint directly from the imagination and not depend on reference material, photographs and drawings.

(Genn) An excellent Montreal artist, Lorne Bouchard, who passed away a few years ago, told me there were three sources for his inspiration. They were reference material, location work, and working directly from the imagination. When alternated day by day and balanced and melded in the creative computer of his mind, he felt he achieved quality results.

On slow days you might try just sitting down and pushing

paint. It's amazing what may materialize out of a free-form start. It's like a Rorschach, suggesting ideas and images.

(*Man*)   I worry constantly about the saleability of my work. I would like to be free of this, because it inhibits the free flow of my interests.

(*Genn*)   Although this path is a minefield of potential pro-belems – you might try letting someone else worry about the saleability of your work. A friend of mine is a well known bird painter. His first wife ran his business for him. In his studio there was a blackboard to the left of the door as he entered every morning, and on that blackboard she would write 'chickadees' or 'Canada geese', or whatever was in high demand in New York. He would go to his easel and do what was written. One day he came into the studio to find 'chickadees' on the board, and he didn't feel like doing them. He realized that he never really did want to do what she told him. He walked out of the studio, climbed into his motor-home, drove to the bank and withdrew ten thousand dollars and she hasn't seen him since. He has subsequently married another woman who will never become his manager, he paints more than ever, doesn't worry about what will sell, and they are very happy.

(*Man*)   When I was younger I used to fiddle a lot, and I drove my parents crazy, but now I realize that play is vital, and I try to make my work into play.

(*Genn*)   Good idea. As artists we realize that our work is play. It's O.K. to play. Guiltless play. Noel Coward said, 'Work is more fun than fun.' Leonard Bernstein, two years before he died, said, 'I have no regrets, but please just give me a little more time to play with my music.'

(*Man*)   I have had great satisfaction in letting my grand-children work with my paints. For their benefit and for mine.

(*Genn*)   Children are valuable for the lessons they teach us. 'The child is father of the man,' said William Wordsworth.

(*Woman*)   What, in your opinion, is the best way to become professional? Should I go to art school?

(*Genn*)   Here's a suggestion. At some time in your life, late or early, take six months, and go to your room. Eliminate social activities and mundane obligations. Get the cooperation of those around you. Ask your partner to make his or her own meals. With concentration I guarantee you will make progress and gain direction in your work. Two or three months into the exercise you will find that you are standing on your own shoulders. Your companions will be books and your own creativity. Six months of a lifetime is not too much to ask, and it's a joy to do it.

(Woman)   The interference from outside is endless.

(Genn)   That interference should be minimized. You may have to save up to get such a clear period in your life. When I was in my late twenties I decided that the time had come to get myself together. I rented a studio, which was a humble upstairs room, ten by ten feet, on Pender Street in Vancouver. I worked and slept there. I dined on tea and rice. I became celibate. I had a lovely girlfriend when I went on this retreat, and she used to come and knock on the door, and I would stand back where she couldn't see me, and I could see her blond hair through the rumply glass in the window. She was lovely like an impressionist painting in that glass. Eventually she stopped coming to my door, and one day she went away for the last time and married a druggist. I can't believe I had such character in those days.

Sometimes I thought I was going nuts. The studio was right across the water from the nine-o'clock-gun. Every evening I would get ready for the bang to go off. When it did I told myself that my head was okay again. I used to divide the day into two parts: before and after the gun.

It was through this cathartic experience that day by day I could feel my work getting better. I painted over six hundred paintings in that hermitage. I burned most of them, but some showed promise, and some were great, and when I came down those rickety stairs for the last time I knew for sure that I loved to paint and would make a life in art.

(Woman)   Your timing was fortunate, though. In defense of other people who have commitments, or children, it is very hard to take that sort of time.

(Genn)   I've heard that before. Emily Carr did it when she was in her fifties. She didn't have children, but she did keep a monkey, and sheep-dogs, and she had a boarding house to run. She was by no means well off. Mary Roberts Rinehart had a job as a nurse, six kids, an alcoholic unemployed husband, and she wanted to write. She did it by setting the alarm-clock for three A.M. Things were easier by the time she was into her third novel, and she ended up writing fifty of them, and plays as well.

(*Man*)   It's a good idea to have a lofty, north-lit studio.

(*Genn*)   Ideally, yes. But a modest studio can work for you too. Just so everything is in its place. I've seen some wonderful work done in a well organized space under the basement stairs.

I visited the home of Dylan Thomas in Laugharne, Wales. The 'boat house,' as it's called, stands as Thomas left it – the rooms where he and Caitlin scrapped furnished as before. Up on the lane which leads down to the boat house is the sanctuary where he did most of his writing. It's a tiny converted garage, painted blue, suitable originally for something as small as an Austin Nippy. Its window looks between the trees at a narrow and uninteresting view of the estuary below. There is a spartan table and a chair facing the window, a bottle with a candle in it, notepaper, some pencils, a few books scattered here and there on wobbly shelves. On the wall, tucked between the studs, a calendar, several posters, train and bus tickets, and a few photographs.

As I looked at this modest building, the creative space of one of the greatest writers of our century, I could see, just as freedom is most on the mind of those confined to dungeons, imagination can fly from humble, quiet, unstimulating places.

I like Annie Dillard's remark: "One wants a room with no view, so imagination can meet memory in the dark."

Speaking of garages – Walt Disney's first studio, where Mickey Mouse was born, was a garage in Burbank.

(*Man*)   I only work on commissions. If I know I'm not going to get paid for doing something, I don't do it. That brings out the child in me, and I make a good living.

(*Genn*)   Do you enjoy doing your work?

(*Man*)   If I'm getting paid, yes.

(*Man*)   Mr. Genn, the public relates to your work. Why?

(*Genn*)   In the popular jargon; it's accessible. The work that pleases me also pleases others. That's lucky. Some artists project more angst and misery in their work, and they have a more difficult time. My work generally reflects the positive and the beautiful, and the public relates to that. This is not a calculated plan, it's just the way the work comes out. Furthermore, I'm not sure of the secret of success, but I do know that the secret of failure is to try to please everybody.

(Man) Does the world and its problems influence your work?

(Genn) Sometimes. I have done work which has been called socially conscious. Generally I see my role as accentuating the positive, and being curious as to where the muse will take me.

(Man) I think one needs a degree of fanaticism to get the best out of one's self.

(Genn) Fanatics toil ceaselessly for their causes, close their minds to critics, and keep the faith with a singleminded and purposeful dedication. Non-fanatics on the other hand, work intermittently with no particular sense of mission, listen to their critics, and diversify their directions. Something can be learned from both extremes. Becoming a fanatic, if only for an hour or a day is a useful exercise. A method of achieving wild enthusiasm is to act wildly enthusiastic. Often, a growing and beautiful love-affair develops quite automatically.

A valuable exercise is to write yourself some lines to define your potential fanaticism. You could choose something like, "I extract variety from gradations", or "I will paint the family of man in all its richness." You tailor the lines for yourself, know what you want, learn your lines, and act them out.

A friend came into the studio one day, looked at the painting on my easel, and said, "My goodness that has a lot of 'Zeus-energy'."

The Zeus I knew was the chief god of Greek mythology. He dashed around Olympus, mating with various goddesses, fathering muses. I looked at the painting. It was confident, energetic, joyful, handsome, well formed, colourful, powerful. I knew what he meant. My painting reflected the way I felt that day. 'I *feel* Zeusal,' I said to him. Another day when my friend phoned and asked me what I was doing I told him I was 'Zeusing around.'

(Man) What about drinking and painting?

(Genn) Don't overlook the possibilities of alcohol. Drink gives some sort of temporary re-alignment of brain cells and relaxes away mundane cares brought on by domesticity or economics. It's also a short-cut to child-like attitudes and right-brain insights. I am not recommending drunkeness, but when it happens use your intoxication to see ingrained pedestrianisms, and let it help you to magic and further possibilities. A pass through the studio late at night after a party can pay valuable dividends in the morning. Judge your work in progress from the loft of your altered state.

If you drink and paint at the same time you will be confident at first, then you will amaze yourself with your speed and facility, but in the morning your vanity will likely have you start another bonfire.

(Man) Sometimes I just don't have any desire to get on with my work. Do you have an antidote for that?

(Genn) The most important quality that you can bring to your work is desire. We have to ask ourselves what it is that causes some people to achieve excellence, while others settle into a mediocre complacency. One wellspring of excellence which artists sometimes admit is condition, the desire to rise from the condition of poverty to the condition of wealth, for example. This person is said to have drive. Poverty sees wealth as a worthwhile goal.

Artists often have an ambiguous attitude toward wealth. They sometimes don't trust it – but it is the bringer of freedom.

A terrible spectre that inhibits desire and haunts artists is "it has all been done before." Furthermore, "what's the use?" and "it won't be appreciated," are two nasty gargoyles that look over our shoulders whether we are cooks or kings.

I find it's a good plan to focus on the idea that unique art is always unique. That's why it is worthwhile to excel yourself every time you break out a new canvas. If the work pleases you there is a good chance it will eventually please someone else. It is important to trust in your uniqueness.

Another wellspring of excellence is the desire to compete. Seeing good work, knowing what is good about it, and then competing with it stimulates more good work. I find it useful to keep good work around to refer to. You will set higher standards for yourself. If you push yourself up to it, you may very well exceed it.

Another great wellspring is egocentrism. You don't have to be unpleasant about it, but you can be a 'demigod,' or a big one, like Zeus.

Artists should be exhibitionists. There is a wonderful feeling when you walk into your own exhibition. You see the work as a true extension of yourself. Win or lose, your interests have led you to an accumulation of your personal expression, signed lower right, mounted to best advantage. It's a minor monument, and you know there will be more monuments to come. If you would achieve your heart's desire, you should never stop chipping away at your statue.

(*Woman*)   How do you feel about commissions? Do they interfere with your normal work. They do for me.

(*Genn*)   Commissions can be detrimental to natural flow. At the present time I have about thirty incomplete commissions. This is the highest amount I have ever had. I practically always say 'yes' to commissions. I never say 'when'.

I was requested to do a portrait of a well known beautiful woman. She wanted to be done with her cats. I phoned and asked her how many cats she had. She said, "Nine." I have never done cats well. Dogs I can do. Pussycats are not on my fun list. Then one morning I woke up with a strange and uncontrollable urge to paint cats. I phoned the beautiful woman, and we met later that day. It took me two days to catch all the cats and photograph them. I came to know the cats on a first name basis. The woman's name was Arletta, and the cats were April, Alexandra, Abe, Axiom, Andree, Ambrose, Axminster, Amsterdam, and Ajax. The painting turned out to be a lot of fun. I think I did a rather good job on those cats – one of them that I was unable to get to know, was painted going out the door. I learned something about painting cats, and came to know a bit about the mystery of their personalities.

(*Woman*)   When you accept commissions, how much freedom do you request from the buyer? Some of my customers complain they didn't get what they expected.

(*Genn*)   You want to maintain your own vision and integrity, but you want to satisfy. Here's what I do: I explain the program to the customer. In my case, I take a lot of photos, study them, and develop some ideas, sizes formats, etc. Then I phone them and discuss what I have in mind. I tell them the exact price, usually giving them a choice of three sizes or poses that I like. They have a pretty good idea of what they are going to get. I often fax them a rough, and they generally reply right away to go ahead. I don't believe in making the rough too accurate. It should be a 'rough rough rough'. This leaves latitude to play.

Producing a quality likeness is difficult. I tell them that if they don't like it they don't have to pay me, but that I will keep the work. I request an opportunity to try again in a few months or a year. A couple of times I have been taken up on it.

You may have to fib a bit when you are painting portraits. I admire John Singer Sargent, who could make his subjects more elegant than they were, and yet he is reported to have produced excellent likenesses.

(Woman)   I have found a good way to bring out my child is to put on a mask and a childish costume when I paint. It gives me confidence.

(Genn)   When you put on a mask you temporarily take on the persona of a different character. This idea is the key to a useful concept. While I was painting in Ireland last year I heard a radio interview with a man who had written a book called *The Way of the Actor.* His point was that we can all learn from actors, who are able to change their personalities to materialize the characters they wish to portray. The qualities become their own. I bought myself a funny green hat and pretended I was a leprechaun and painted a lot of little tiny paintings.

If you want to be an insurance adjuster, you act insurance adjuster. If you want to be an artist, you act artist. A clown costume could have a liberating effect on the work of a lot of us.

(Woman)   I find when I take off my glasses, I don't see very well and I paint fresher.

(Genn)   Softer vision produces softer paintings and helps you to see the 'big picture.' in both your reference and in the work you are producing. Skilled artists with glasses take them on and off during the process. Half-frames and bi-focals are handy for this.

(Woman)   I'm blind in one eye.

(Genn)   You might be interested in a book called *The World Through Blunted Sight,* by Patrick Trevor-Roper. It deals with the influence on artists of a wide range of conditions such as myopia,

astigmatism, mind-altering drugs, and personal habits. El Greco's figures, for example, with their curious and slanting elongation has often been attributed to astigmatism. It is also possible that his distortions are due to the rigid positioning of the right handed artist vis-a-vis a high-easeled canvas. Interestingly, his pencil sketches and small works don't show the same distortions.

Blindness in one eye may be worth exploring as a creative tool. As Confucious said, "An inconvenience is an unrecognized opportunity."

Hour 3

Planning for Quality

(Genn)   How do we plan our hours and days to achieve quality? I like to say that quality is always in style. When I was starting out as a painter I knew there were artists who survived and even flourished, and I felt that if I could just bring quality to my work, then I too could flourish.

We must search our minds for a definition of quality. We learn that contemporary public galleries would likely not want anything that we in this room could produce. And conversely, there are collectors who would not want anything that the contemporary public galleries could show them. There are orthodoxies in art, just as there are in religion. "Orthodoxy is my doxy; heterodoxy is another man's doxy," said William Warburton to Lord Sandwich. So, keeping in mind that quality depends on a personal viewpoint, how do we go about getting quality work out of ourselves?

(Man)   Original ideas.

(Genn)   You feel more comfortable and confident with your own original ideas.

(Woman)   Planning. Preparing your ideas, your colour, your composition. Knowing where you are going before you start.

(Genn)   On ambitious or complicated work it is a good idea to do decent roughs. Make at least some of your mistakes in your rough. You will see that you are going to have trouble with the foreground, or that you will need something more over here, that sort of thing. The rough is a secret contract between you and the work, and it will help your final quality. While there is something to be said for wading right into the work for spontaneity and flow, by and large

you will increase quality by planning.

(*Woman*)   I find quality comes to me when I just let go, let my intuition flow. I do not like to impose demands on the canvas, or the clay, or necessarily where the drawing is going to take me. I like to let it just work itself out. I relax, and I don't push it.

(*Genn*)   I have a couple of two-string kites. They are zen-like to fly, and if you don't know what you are doing they can pull a grown man right off the ground. They have their own knowledge and rhythm, and when the kite wants to take a turn I cooperate with it, and let it do its thing. That way the exercise becomes effortless, beautiful, and fun.

(*Woman*)   I like to work in both a realistic and an abstract manner. I let my feelings tell me which way I will paint.

(*Woman*)   For me I feel it is best if I paint something I feel passionate about. That gets me excited.

(*Genn*)   How do you develop passion?

(*Woman*)   When I feel the passion waning in a subject, I move to another. I do landscapes for a while and then I change to wild animals. Sometimes one painting gives me the passion for another.

(*Genn*)   Lawren Harris told me that he felt paintings come out of themselves. Halfway through one you find out what the next one is to be. I find that as I get into a painting I have high hopes, then little by little I begin to see that it is not going to be the masterpiece I thought it would be, and I start putting my hopes into the next work.

But to continue on the idea of developing passion, I would equate passion with enthusiasm. I once read a book by a baseball player who was criticized by the press for being lazy on the field. When he saw this in the sports pages he decided to have 'ants in his pants' and jump around a lot, looking active and enthusiastic. The press started calling him 'Fire-Ball,' but, most importantly, his game improved.

(*Woman*)   When I look at my work in a half finished state for a while, I become enthusiastic to get on with it, find out more about it, and fix what's wrong with it.

(*Man*)   In my work I can't plan for quality. Quality happens or it doesn't happen. It's accidental. I work in watercolour, and plans don't always work.

(Genn)　　Is part of your plan to throw some of them away?

(Man)　　More than some.

(Man)　　I believe in allowing myself no compromises. I go to a lot of trouble to get it right.

(Genn)　　Jane Hopkins said, "Genius is the infinite capacity for taking pains." I was looking at an eagle that Robert Bateman had painted, and it looked natural and beautiful. He told me that he had scraped off and re-painted the head four times to bring it to where it was.

I am sorry to say there are times when most of us say, "That will be good enough," and it isn't.

(Woman)　　I feel it is unfortunate in art that there is no way to measure what is good and what is bad.

(Genn)　　You can tell a good accountant from a bad accountant by his balance, or a doctor by how many dead he has among his clients. It bothers me that you see ads in the classified that say, "I would like to thank Dr. Jones and the staff at the hospital for the very good care they gave my late husband."

But it's hard to put your finger on what's good in art. I once saw a sign in a commercial gallery that said: "If you like it, it's a great painting."

(Woman)　　Perhaps quality comes from the very being of the artist, and his character.

(Genn)　　Agreed. Our world suffers from a character drought. We have talent, we have capability, we have desire, we have wonderful equipment, but we don't have a lot of character. It is a rare and fragile flower. Bismarck said, "Politics ruins the character." With this in mind we should stay at arms' length from governments, boards, dealers, commerce, agencies. It is advice I have not always taken.

Artists with character are the ones who think things through and are able to take a strong, even agressive, position. 'My strength is as the strength of ten, because my heart is pure.' That sort of thing. Also, I think artists with character, though they may be frustrated, are happier. John Ruskin said: "In order that people may be happy in their work, these three things are needed: They must be fit for it. They must not do too much of it. And they must have a sense of success in it."

(Woman) With regard to the lack of passion, I have found that if I do something completely different, say with pastels or in drawing, I will eventually find my direction in paint for that day. I do purposeless play, and it moves me into a creative place.

(Genn) You try a separate but related activity for a while, and this generates your direction.

(Woman) I feel those are simply exercises in enabling you to get within yourself.

(Woman) I find my happiest work arises when I get into the kind of a 'high' that joggers experience. I feel good about the paintings, they are special to me, but I can't say that such a frame of mind improves their quality.

(Genn) I believe there are two main practical lines which generate work. Some work comes out of style, and some comes from ideas. The photographer Richard Avedon said, "Start with a style and you are in chains, start with an idea and you are free." A lot of artists start with style. They go into the world and look for things on which to inflict their style. Other artists start with an idea and find ways and means to illustrate that idea. Pablo Picasso, for example, took the idea of 'beauty and the beast' and in the most casual and varied way he drew that idea: bulls' heads, masks, threatening figures, and delicate women in compromising situations. They are clumsily drawn, but the idea jumps out at you. Many of us are hung up on pretty scenes which are pleasant vehicles for our style, but which do not have any particular idea behind them. We are content to clone something that has already been done to death. Daily, we are examples of Marshall McLuhans' observation that art is a rear-vision mirror.

At the same time art requires a style force – an element of style that propels the creativity, the look, the myth. Without it there is no art. The cathedral depends on the elements of stained glass, arch, pillar, tomb, painting – reflecting the upward look of religion as style force.

Here's another way of looking at it. Take as an example the first two lines of a limerick:

There was a young man of St John's,
Who had an affair with some swans.

This concept didn't come about through the observation of a student of St John's College, Cambridge, who sodomized with large web-footed swimming birds of the genus Cygnus. It came about because of the need to find a word that rhymed with St John's. The style of the limerick, and in particular the need to have a rhymed couplet, is the style force that produces this extraordinary image. Without the need for rhyme the story might have gone – "A young man from St John's College wished to make love to his girlfriend as frequently as possible." How ordinary. How artless.

(Man)   Some people equate quality with the time you put into something. This is unfortunate.

(Genn)   When people ask me how long it took to paint something, I tell them thirty years, and they understand. Artists must have no guilt about producing work in short order, and they must learn to stop when overworking begins. It is better to leave a work ten percent unfinished than to overwork it one percent.

(Woman)   I am one of those artists who likes to start with an idea and work it out in many ways. And when I show these to a gallery they tell me to stick to a single style. They want to promote a single image or a look.

(Genn)   Versatility is not always in style. Galleries seem to want specialists. This is a really pervasive problem, and here's how I deal with it. I was working in the U.S. Southwest, in Ontario, and on the West Coast of Canada. My work and my interests were wide-ranging, so I sent my work from the areas of my work to dealers in those areas. That way I was able to be versatile in my work and consistent with my dealers. After I had been doing this for a decade or so I found that the more sophisticated collectors would notice my work in different areas, and realize that I was capable of more. So rather than people coming to my shows and wanting more of the same, they came with the question, "What is he doing now?" And the result was that the advanced clientele took the conservative dealers along with them. Artists like Picasso made a lifetime of variety

out of this idea. We are all familiar with his periods. He was consistent in his ability to change. The way to do this is to explore the possibilities in one area together with those in another. Simultaneity. It is like moving up a pawn when you play chess. You can also enrich your work by putting it on the back burner for a while. Some artists call this "moodeling".

I sometimes say to myself that if I was any kind of artist I should be able to keep painting my own back yard. One time I had a show booked in Edmonton, Alberta, and the dealer phoned and asked what it was going to be about. I said Brittany. I had been there for the summer and I had lots of things painted around Pont-Aven, right where Paul Gauguin and Vincent Van Gogh had worked, and I was really enthused by it all. The dealer said, "Robert, we can't sell French paintings in Edmonton." I sent them anyway. As it worked out there were enough customers who were following my progress to make the show a sell-out. Strangely, a few months after the show the dealer phoned my studio and asked if I would do another Brittany show, but I gave him Connemara next time, after a trip to Eire, and he said that definitely wouldn't work, but it was successful too.

(*Woman*) When we see your work we always recognize your style. I feel your particular style carries through your work, no matter where you go, and it gives you your authority and your continuity.

(*Genn*) I think that what you are getting at is that I am one of those artists who is stuck on style. I accept that. I wish that I was better at working from ideas. Try to do what I say and not what I do. However, you are right, your style, if you paint enough, will develop automatically.

(*Woman*) But if you were more idealistic in your painting right now, and worked with your ideas more, you might not be selling as well as you are. You might be taking this course instead of giving it.

(*Genn*) I have to protest that my work does not sell that well. I paint a lot and distribute well. I get a lot of mileage by setting my work around my studio and saying that this or that painting would probably go best in this or that city. I have about thirty dealers. Many of them I have never met, but when paintings are finished I am able to make a small commercial decision which is in favor of this or that dealer.

With regard to taking this course; I am taking this course. As the lady said, 'How do I know what I think until I hear what I say?' Taking courses like this helps keep me in touch – and humble.

(Woman) There comes a time in our creative life when we want to see if it is possible to get green-feedback from what we love to do. Most of us don't enjoy selling our own work. It's difficult. We have to find people who will do it for us, and who are motivated. What is the best way to approach a gallery?

(Genn) The acceptable way to attract dealers is to send slides. There are so many artists now that dealers don't have the time to give interviews to everyone who comes along. It helps to ask a known artist to back you up, to vouch for your quality, seriousness, productivity, reliability, etc. Dealers appreciate artists who deliver when they say they will, and are pleasant and easy to get along with. If the artist does colourful and interesting things in his life, if there are stories that go along with the paintings, so much the better. Sometimes a dealer will reject you because he already has someone who paints in your bailiwick. Perhaps not as well. Try his competition. A good idea is to show work which is nothing like what the dealer has on his walls – then you will be filling a niche for him. When you establish a dealer don't interfere in his territory by selling privately or doing craft-shows or malls, etc. Protect him and go for the long term. He, together with other dealers, is the business partner who can eventually get more for your paintings than they are worth. You can't do that on your own.

Here's another suggestion: Go for galleries in other cities, in other areas. There's nothing worse than being a 'local artist.' Send paintings of the Okanagan to Montreal, or of Taos Pueblo to New York. In other words, send the work of an area you know and love to a distant city.

(Man) It seems to me that when you manage to get your work into a gallery and your paintings are too cheap, they don't sell, and also when they are too expensive. If a work is excellent, is it a good idea to ask a higher price for it?

(Genn) I don't think you should advance the price of a painting because you think more of it, or because you have put more work into it. Paintings by living artists should be priced according to size.

In the eye of the public every one of us has a perceived value. The work has to be good, but it also must be cheap. What I mean by that is that an Andrew Wyeth is cheap at $20,000.00 and an unknown, neophite artist is expensive at the same price. Price-range is based on factors such as the quality that can be achieved, years of commitment, age, and, of course, whether an artist is or is not dead.

If you are a genius, your work can be expensive right from the start. I've never met anyone to whom this applies. Your prices should start at an affordable level, with room for price expansion. It's traditional that the price of art goes up, which makes it unpleasant to bring down.

Since I first began painting I have advanced my prices ten percent a year, with a couple of years at twenty percent, and one year not at all. In my opinion prices should be slightly 'supra-inflationary,' that is, slightly ahead of inflation, so there is a small investment value built into them. My prices change on the same day each year, April the first.

The price of paintings does not have a lot to do with supply and demand. They should be perceived as rare, but they eventually become more valuable because they are more expensive. It is unfortunate that dealers would rather have paintings that sell easily for three thousand dollars than ones that are hard to sell for three hundred. That's the rub. Wall-space is an expensive commodity.

(Woman)   The investment factor spoils the market for the beginning artist.

(Genn)   I agree, but I should add that there is nothing like buying a penny stock and seeing it go through the roof. I really appreciate my early collectors who had faith and encouraged me when I first got started. I give special attention to them. But the sideroads are strewn with the bodies of artists who advanced their prices too quickly. There is no secondary market for much of their work, and it is this market which really establishes prices.

(Woman)   What's the secondary market?

(Genn)   Auction Houses, classified advertisements, works resold through dealers other than your own.

(Man)   As an artists' manager there is no way that I will accept an artist who has been painting for two years and who wants to jump into the big time. I like artists who have paid their dues.

(Genn)   What do you say about the super-novas that burst on the scene, then disappear to their cabanas in the Caribbean, never to be seen again?

(Man)   They are a disgrace to the art community. Unfortunately we have no way of controlling them. In this day of the media, bad art can be promoted in high quality, often government funded, magazines. This goes to the heads of inadequate artists, and creates a temporary and unjustifiable bubble. The old idea of craftsmanship has been clouded by the new possibilities of hype.

(Woman)   It seems to me that the shoe ought to be on the other foot. It should be the artists who tell the galleries what to hang. Why don't artists say to the dealer "Buy my work and do what you like with it." Artists who put their work out on consignment should have more say.

·   *(Genn)*   There are dealers around that want to buy your work. These dealers generally don't last. The reason for this is that they gradually build a collection of the poorer paintings. Dealers with staying power understand economics.

When a dealer takes paintings on consignment, which I'm sure is the better way, the paintings stay in the hands of the artist until they go out into the world. The artist then has the option to take the work back into his own archive, destroy it, or perhaps give it to a university, government institution, or charity. The artist is the best person to rationalize it. Also, dealers who own your work, can release your work into the market at less favorable times in an economic cycle.

A way around this has been 'artist-run galleries'. Artists get together and present their works in a location and either sell one another's or pay someone else to do it. In my experience these arrangements don't generally work either. Problems arise: ego problems, division of labour problems, money problems. I believe artists should be artists and dealers should be dealers. Artists should not be in the front trenches, taking flak, listening to opinion, and defending themselves.

(Woman)   Customers think they should pay less when they are buying direct from artists.

(Genn)   That's another good reason for staying out of dealing.

(Woman) I think the education of children in art is important so they can grow up with an understanding of the subject.

(Woman) We can't wait that long.

(Woman) Children should be taken to art galleries and taught to have a good eye.

(Genn) Children in thousands are led through the public art galleries, and they are shown new things and often told what they should like. Docents click and count them through with clickers, and galleries rack up points and get grants for doing so. Is this a good idea?

(Woman) I think it creates artistic confusion and ignorance.

(Woman) I think it's wonderful.

(Woman) I think it is unfortunate that a lot of our young people are growing up without getting a broad idea of what quality is.

(Man) I think commercial artists do the best art.

(Genn) Sign shops, advertising agencies, and printing firms are a common source for the development of fine artists. There has been extensive documentation of this phenomenon. The great architects of the Gothic cathedrals emerged from the ranks of the stone masons. With one exception, all members of the Canadian Group of Seven worked for Grip Ltd, a Toronto Printing establishment. Our toughest competition is likely to come from the commercial world, and not from the art school world or the teaching world, as popularly believed. Why? Commercial people have often learned craftsmanlike and workmanlike habits, respect for deadlines, respect for the clock. They know their materials. They have the worker's edge. It has been my experience that the commercial artist's greatest problem when they come to fine art is accepting the direction (or lack of direction) of the new and wishy-washy boss – themselves.

(Woman) Don't you think there should be more government funding for the arts?

(Genn) It might be possible that government funding, and the expectation of it, puts an unnatural spin on the development of talent. As it stands education is already highly subsidised – to the point where it is considered by many to be an unalienable right.

During Centennial year in British Columbia we artists were given a big bun-toss in the city of Prince George. Chuck and Di were there. I sat right behind them on the podium. He didn't even wave his ears at me, but she eventually turned and gave me a shy smile. During the ceremony legions of young artists marched into the arena. It was like the procession at the Olympic Games. They carried placards; 'The Painters,' 'The Potters,' 'The Sculptors,' 'The Actors.' My goodness, the actors, they kept on coming – hundreds – no, thousands of them. Could the acting schools be responsible for turning out this many thesbians? To hold them, all the world would have to be a stage. I began to think of motion picture projects with casts of thousands that would give them all a job.

When the Prince spoke he said that talent was uncommonly common in the colonies, and that we struck him as having a very bright future indeed.

(Woman)   I subscribed to an avant-garde art magazine for a while, and I found most of the artistry was in the write-ups.

(Genn)   There is a wonderful little book called *The Painted Word,* by Tom Wolfe. The same who wrote *Bonfire of the Vanities,* and *The Right Stuff.* You can read it in an evening. He says that what is happening is that art is not exhibited in New York unless it can be talked and written about. No one can criticize the rendering of a hand or a likeness anymore. That has become banal among the critics. But they can talk handsomely and long about what is 'beyond criticism.' For these critics acceptable art has its potential verbosity 'built in.' Furthermore, art, like product design, has fallen prey to 'the cult of the new.' In his opinion it is a fresh case of *'The Emperor's New Clothes.'*

(Woman)   My husband and I have just returned from the National Gallery of Canada, where we saw the 'Voice of Fire,' which our government has seen fit to invest in for $1.8 million. We found it lacking in virtues. You can see that it was done with a roller, and you can see the taped edges. It has no depth or mystery. It seemed to us to be a great big piece of nothing. But it fooled the experts.

(Woman)   Experts are the greatest of fools.

(Genn)   Looking at the painting from my perspective, Barnett Newman's passion was underwhelming. However, the

authorities that the government hires to choose our public art don't agree with me.

Artists themselves can be remarkably honest. Pablo Picasso remarked: "Since the advent of Cubism, I have fed these fellows what they wanted and satisfied the critics with all the ridiculous ideas that passed through my head. The less they understood me, the more they admired me. Through amusing myself with these farces, I became celebrated and rich. When I am alone, I do not have the effrontery to consider myself an artist, not in the grand meaning of the word. Titian, Rembrandt and Goya were the great painters. I am only a public clown, a mountebank."

(Man)   Robert, I would be interested to hear your comments on the trend to prints. Does this hurt the fine art market? Are prints art?

(Genn)   We must distinguish between photo-litho reproductions and prints made by other more 'hands on' methods: serigraphy, stone-lithography, engraving, mezzotint, wood-block. Each of these types of print-making is an art in itself. Art, to be of lasting value, should have quality, rarity, and permanence. Many photo-lithos have quality in their original composition. If I cannot afford an original that I love, a print will have to do. It is in the next two criteria that photo-lithos begin to fall down. Any rarity associated with them is artificial. Editions now seem to go into the thousands. But it is in the area of permanence that I have the most trouble. It is simply not brilliant to invest in something that no matter how glazed and varnished, will fade and change colour when subjected to direct sunlight. Even in moderate light photo-lithos can change in a few years.

Further, the print phenomenon has come and gone, it is a cyclical game. New generations come along and make it happen. With very few exceptions none of the very well produced and in their time expensive prints from the nineteenth century are worth very much today. Obviously, the phenomenon has more to do with greed and investment than with art. Our culture has come to such a state that collectors of prints become traders and expect quick profits, often in weeks or months. The print phenomenon exists because walls are still being built faster than works of lasting value are being made to go on them.

(Man)   The main art of the photo-litho houses is cutting the deal with the often young and unknown artist, and when that deal becomes too expensive for the publisher they drop the artist. They are seldom interested in important artists.

(Woman)   I have had some experience with print publishers lately. They liked my work, but told me that they can't print what they like, only what they know will sell. Right now primary colours are in.

(Genn)   As the wise man said when he was asked for a statement that would apply to all situations: 'And this too shall pass.'

(Woman)   How do you produce your serigraphs?

(Genn)   Making prints by hand is more satisfying to me than sending a painting to a printer to be reproduced. Also, cooperation and consultation are important in serigraphy (or silk-screen), and make the exercise enjoyable. A lot of the credit for my work goes to my assistants with whom I work closely. Here's how we do it.

Our printmaking is largely experimental. We may start with a painting, or we may develop a motif from a drawing. My screens have been traditionally hand cut, although sometimes the images are drawn directly on the screen. Lately we have been trying to use a photographic method of making the image.

It is exciting to see the proofs as each color is produced. Building colour on colour, they give the direction for the colours that follow. We print between four and twelve colours. Editions range between thirty and ninety. Each edition takes a couple of weeks. There is no attempt to make a print look like a specific painting. Prints are their own art.

Each colour is run separately. Some are transparent glazes, some are opaques, and others are what we call semi-opaques. The most difficult are the gradations, that is, two separate coloured inks that go through the screen at the same time and blend during the run.

It is like a game of chess in which the outcome is unknown. Move by move you work toward a winning conclusion. Sometimes a daring gambit is a failure. Sometimes, in exasperation, you simply 'move up a pawn,' that is, make a simple decision that will have a known result. Print-making wins you over with its complexity.

Hour 4

Motivation

(Genn)   The question often arises regarding the value of higher education in the fine arts. During the break some of you were expressing the feeling that working within a rigid curriculum might be difficult for you at this time. Others of you thought you needed to go back to basics and learn some skills and techniques. I guess my message is that no matter what your inclination, you should try to operate as a rugged individualist.

Alexander Pope said, 'A little learning is a dangerous thing.' I believe that one should be first of all a working person and secondly a talking person. We must contemplate, but we must not take too much satisfaction in intellectualizing our work. Mark Twain had a name for people like this. He called them 'mugwumps,' that is, persons educated beyond their intelligence and capabilities. The problem as I see it with many art schools is that their graduates are artistically literate, but not many are artists.

There was a time when the kind of work we like to do was taught in schools, and before that a system of apprenticeship was in effect. Today many master artists tend to guard their own, hard won knowledge. But these days we have wonderful books that were not available to the old masters. Our dens can now house the Louvre, and the best educator we can employ is our own curiosity. Many of the skills we need to learn are skills we can learn for ourselves.

In the arts, the diplomas, medals, and testimonials that count most are the ones we award ourselves.

(Woman)   What we were talking about is that you seem to have a broad education, and this has helped you get where you are.

(Genn)   It is so much easier to learn and grow when you get up in the morning and ask yourself, 'What do I want to learn today?' It is rather like Thoreau's deciding to find out everything there was

to know about beans. He did it through the seasons, among the beanrows, beside his pond.

Much as I would like to say that I have found artists to be of superior intellect, I don't think you can generalize. Sometimes the plainest thinkers turn out to be very good painters. But these plain thinkers have a secret, and there is a parable to describe it:

Catch a bee in a jar and release it from a high place and watch which way it goes – then go in that direction – then catch another and another and do the same until the honey tree is found.

Let's talk about motivation. During this segment we are going to explore ways that get us started and keep us going. What makes Pablo run?

(Man)   We work because we have an inborn need to be busy and make things.

(Woman)   I do it out of love.

(Genn)   Kahlil Gibran said: "Work is love made visible."

(Man)   I do it for deadlines.

(Woman)   I get motivated by talking to other artists and seeing what they are doing.

(Genn)   I know of places where artists meet together every night, and drink and talk, and whine with each other, and share their misery. And I think that in the long run they wear each other down and often destroy their need to work. I've found that most of the better artists are loners. They share a camaraderie through the brotherhood of art, but they stick to themselves.

Working together is another matter. Sometimes you can be lucky enough to establish a working relationship with another artist who takes away the loneliness, particularly in travel and outdoor work. I had a friend by the name of Jack Hambleton, who has since passed on. We had the same metabolism on the road; we produced about the same amount of work in a day. There was a kind of amusing competition between us. Jack sometimes aggravated me with his speed. My unsettled chopping and changing bothered him. We made a deal when we were driving that whoever called 'stop' had a veto over the other. One time we were driving across a busy bridge in Spain and Jack said 'stop' and I stopped. Traffic swerved around us. Horns blared. His little folding stool came out, and right there he went to work on a small painting. This sort of commitment helped to commit me. We were in mild competition and I think we showed off to one another too.

(Woman)   I find painting is a form of meditation, and I find a lot of answers while I'm painting. I also meditate before painting.

(Genn)   There are those who claim meditation unclutters the mind, aids concentration, and builds creativity and personal joy. Many artists seem to benefit from meditation.

The question most often asked by those who are skeptical of meditation is, "If strong emotion and passion are key elements in creation, does the practice of meditation sedate creativity?"

A confirmed meditator told me: "Meditation calms the mind and nervous system and helps to make the emotions pure and clear and strong. Meditation helps us to get in touch with our emotions. Meditation knocks down the barriers that keep us from the full experience of life. Most of us limit our experience out of fear or loss. We dull our minds with tobacco and alcohol, we dull our senses with overloads, loud music and entertainment. We tighten our minds with stress. Meditation dissolves what it is that keeps us from full experience. The more fully we experience, the more fully we are able to participate in the dance of life. And if painting is how we choose to dance, we then become more fulfilled in that endeavor. Fulfillment is ensured on the way as well as on arrival."

Methods which artists seem to favor often involve visualization. These include the visualization of the artist's own signature, small objects in groups generally from one to ten and back again, or colour areas of different shapes.

I have left few stones unturned in my search for new levels of creativity, and my dig into meditation has produced mixed results. Some artists take it seriously. I know an artist who hangs a little sign on her door when she meditates: "Artist at work...do not disturb."

For those who want to follow up on this – there are countless books, groups galore, and an army of willing gurus.

(Woman)   I like to stay highly alert at all times. I depend upon what I see in the real world for motivation. I look out the window and see a cloud and that sets me to work.

(Woman)   Workshops motivate me.

(Genn)   I haven't heard of anyone becoming a boxer by going to prize-fights. You have to be careful attending demonstrations by wizards; they can satisfy the need to be in the milieu, without having to put a brush to a canvas. After a while in workshops we all feel very happy and comfortable together, and it sort of feels like a club. As Groucho said when he was invited to join a club: "Why would I want to join an organization that would encourage a person like myself to become a member?" I have been guilty of doing quite a few workshops but now I think I am sort of like the priest who advises people not to attend church.

(Man)   I think a great motivator is the need for recognition.

(Genn)   Good point. Artists have a need to stand out. They often need appreciation by peers. Some artists need fame and an adoring public. I'm keen on immortality. If the work we do in life has some lasting value and quality, it will carry us on after our passing.

Some people have a deep-seated need to excel, to stand out, even to draw attention. I believe we are earmarked in youth, generally through the encouragement of parents, although sometimes, and just as effectively it seems, as a reaction against parental neglect or even abuse.

Artists frequently report that when they were kids they were the last ones to be chosen for the sports team. They had to find other ways to get their strokes. I believe that most of us artists had a key occurrence that sent us in the direction of art. Psychologists and hypnotists can sometimes dig out this key occurrence.

Add to this the experiences we have through our early education, particularly high school and college. One of the main purposes of an education is to find out what we can't do. When what we are left with is some form of art, then we find it imperative to go with it.

Discovering our strengths and personal qualities such as self-motivation, ambition, need for control and right-brained function helps us to discover our happiest direction. I know some artists who have developed a strong altruistic sense – they are distributors of what they see as calmness, peace, truth and beauty. Others I know have gone to work with a strong personal politic and world view. Ideas and intrinsic outlooks are stronger innovators than the more simplistic concepts that artists often rationalize.

As I said before, love and anger are prime motivators. Love may involve doing something for someone, or just doing it for the love of it. Anger, too, can provide the energy for creativity and productivity, but above it all, artists require egocentricity and a degree of self absorption in order to fly.

(Man)   When I get publicity I get motivated.

(Genn)   Salvador Dali was accused of liking publicity too much, to which he replied, "True, but publicity likes Dali."

(Woman)   My greatest motivators are art books, and reproductions of paintings.

(Genn)   Books are perhaps mankind's greatest invention. They are the source of sources. Sometimes just holding a book I love motivates me.

(Woman)   I have what I call 'idea books.' They generate many good things for me.

(Genn)   How do you state your ideas in your idea book?

(Woman)   Some are quotes. Some are observations, others are just ideas that come to me in my car, my bed, in my dreams. Sometimes I draw. Sometimes I write.

(Genn)   I make idea books too, for example from my last trip to France. This page is from the Toulouse-Lautrec Museum in Albi. Here's one: 'Painting by T-L on hardwood panel with high gloss priming either varnish or shellac. Soft and brushy background subject scraped away, very unfocused; main subject tight and well focused.' Here's one from the road: 'A tall gentleman in Picardy, long nose, black beret, buttoned-up shirt, suspenders, no tie, carrying two baguettes, leaning on a bicycle; roses.'

(Man)   Travel motivates me. It fills me up with new ideas that I have to do something about.

(Man)   Self exploration. When I explore myself I sometimes feel very shallow and indolent, and for some reason that spurs me on.

(Genn)   Excellent point. Writing about the process of inspiration Jean Cocteau suggested, "Inspiration doesn't fall from heaven, but rather in spite of the existence of any positive creative forces.

Inspiration arrives as the result of profound indolence and our incapacity to put to work forces within ourselves. These unknown forces deep within us, burden us until they make us conquer our indolence and the comfort of reality." Thus, when the artist is 'not working' the greatest of creativity may be fulminating within him.

Cocteau says: "I was sick and tired of writing, when one morning after having slept poorly, I awoke with a start and witnessed, as from a seat in a theater, three acts of a play which had wonderful characters, and was so good I found it awesome. Long afterward, I succeeded in writing the play and I discovered the circumstances that made me do it."

(Woman)   That's true. I need to sit around and have a dull time so I can build up the desire to paint.

(Genn)   Professional artists know all about indolence, and the sudden, unexplained illumination that comes afterward. For me the stages after indolence are as follows;

1.   Assembly.
2.   Digestion.
3.   Illumination.
4.   Application.
5.   Evaluation.

(Man)   How do you deal with constant and chronic indolence?

(Genn)   Pay attention to your periods of indolence. They are often the heralds of valuable transitions. The idea is to try to find what it is that is really bothering you. I find that periods of indolence are sprung by something I might have said, an unfulfillable promise, an upcoming show, guilt, or a feeling of discouragement. If you can train yourself to tune into them properly, you can neutralize the cause, and they can help you to focus on your next period – your next direction. Sometimes what you think is bothering you is not the real problem. I have found that the dawn that breaks after a well contemplated period of indolence will practically always lead to a sunny day.

It's a good idea to be indolent for at least twenty minutes every day. Sometimes three or four days of indolence is useful. But chronic indolence – a period of weeks or months is a dangerous vegetation that can lead to the habit of sterility. When you realize you are starting to enjoy the indolence, this is the danger signal, and you must make an effort to move on. Make your indolences quick and easy by digging around in them, and you will thrive again.

When indolence results in a waste of time, it is often caused by misguided work activity. For example, you may be indolent in oils or acrylics, but not in watercolors or drawings. To shake this sort of indolence you must go where your present heart tells you.

The Japanese have a little doll called a 'daruma' which teaches a valuable lesson. It is a round bottomed schmoo-like character that springs to a vertical position no matter how you lay it down.

(Man)   The other arts inspire me: drama, theater, motion pictures, the symphony. Where you see other people excelling. What other people do well really turns me on.

(Woman)   As an artist, when I compare myself to my friends, I find that I see things differently than other people, and I am unique and have a gift, and it makes me want to go and express that unique vision.

(Man)   Success is a good motivator. It tends to make me do more.

(Genn)   It is unfortunate, but if we do not seem to be successful we are inclined to feel there is something wrong with what we are doing. My friend Jack Hambleton used to say, "I love looking for things to paint, and I love painting, and I love framing them and seeing them in a gallery, but more than anything, I love to sell them." That, he felt, completed the circle.

(Woman)   Don't you find that sales are a good motivator?

(Genn)   Contrary to popular belief I try as much as possible to be innocent of the action in the galleries which handle my work. It's been my observation that many successful artists are accused of entrepreneurship, but in reality it's the beginning and barely-surviving artists that pay the most attention to sales.

I feel it is important to separate the joy of work from the receipt of cheques.

Here's my system for motivation. It's a simple one. I enter the studio in the morning with my coffee cup in my hand and I sit in a comfortable chair and take a look at yesterday's works on a secondary easel. There are generally two or three paintings going at the same time, and while they are unfinished they are framed and under a good light. It's the unfinished work which prompts me to start. Things that I thought I was going to have to do, I don't have to do, and things that I didn't know I had to do, I must. When I give my creative mind that overnight rest, and look at the work in retrospect and a sense of surprise, some unexplainable something propels me out of my easy chair, and I take the painting, remove it from its frame and put it on the main easel. I squeeze my paint with joy and go to work. The pump has been primed.

If I do not have anything on my secondary easel there are several backups that can get me going. One is the photo collection. I have a light-table and a slide bank which now contains 165,000 slides. They are filed according to subject matter, and I cruise this for a while to find out if there are any directions there. Sometimes I mix and match and find two or three reference photos that might fit together. Perhaps a figure for the foreground, and a landscape for the background, and a seagull from the seagull file for the sky. This is often how I develop an interest in a subject.

If my creative well is still dry, I read or look at books for a while. I try to look at what I consider top stuff, or the artists that are currently interesting me. Another motivation is sorting through sketches or my older paintings. Sometimes I complete an old one that I had abandoned for lack of patience or enthusiasm, or I see a new way that the subject can be made satisfying. Half-finished paintings from trips are useful in this way.

If I enter the studio and say to myself, 'What do I want to do today?' and the decision is not to do anything, that's all right too. It could be a day for looking, or flying a kite, or other play. Sometimes I get really keen on print-making for a day or so. The important thing is that it is right at the time. I have to really ask myself what is right.

Try not to be driven by demand. Let desire drive you. As Ben Kenobe said to Luke Skywalker, 'Trust the force, Luke.'

A dangerous thing is to have a special blank canvas around that you feel you must fill. It is best to buy a large supply of various sizes, so you are not obliged to paint on any one of them, and when you have an idea, or a design, you can ask yourself which size would be best. You must always try to get the right scale for your concept. Not anticipating the scale needed can cause trouble. The common problem is that the subject is too small for the canvas.

In my studio a smaller painting is generally produced in a couple of hours. It gets further touched and thought about for two or three days. It is then stewed about for a month. Sometimes quite a bit more is done to it. Then it is signed, varnished and shipped away. Different artists have different systems. Some find it better to make paintings one at a time and get the feeling of completion. Sending them away from the studio frees up the spirit for the next ones.

Another way to self-motivate is to simply begin using your easel. Just folding out one of those French easels – especially out of doors on a nice day – seems to invite getting started. With the equipment there it's a shame not to use it – especially inasmuch as it's so precise – so nicely made.

Those French easels have some disadvantages of course. They become rickety with age – I've worn out three of them. Also, have you ever tried folding one up and putting it away when you've been drinking? Mr Bean couldn't have done it better.

What frequently motivates me to outdoor work is an easel of my own design – I call it the "art-dog". It's specially built to my specifications and does everything I need. Light and strong – it has wheels – and can be taken virtually anywhere – I can even tow it with my bike. It opens up and is ready to go in seconds. It has features like a comfortable seat with a backrest, a maul-stick, an attachment for a patio umbrella – and other features. It becomes such a nice place to be that I can't help being motivated. I like to tell myself it's not just an easel – it's a way of life.

(Woman)   Do you send what you think are only the very best to the galleries?

(Genn)   I try to have as much integrity as possible. Goodness knows it would be nice to always make 'tens'. But I am lucky if I get a 'nine'. I try not to send anything below a 'six' to a gallery. There is sometimes a lot of pressure to send work, any work, and at these times I show my neurotic tendencies.

(Man)   I find galleries are loaded with reproductions, and I have been saying to them that they should take originals.

(Genn)   Galleries that sell prints and reproductions are not always able to sell originals. Galleries that sell originals often have a hard time with prints. There are two different markets.

(Woman)   How do print galleries work?

(Genn)   Print galleries work on a different system than galleries that sell originals and represent artists. Print galleries are very often required to pay within thirty days for the prints from the big houses like Millpond Press or New York Graphics. Their mark-up is consequently higher. They can be left with editions that don't sell. They are often asked to accept quotas, or limited in what they can buy. They are part of the team of a "controlled rarity distribution investment game." Print dealers often have a peculiar shakiness when dealing with original artists, too. Even though they are fine folks they sometimes don't seem to have the same confidence as gallery people. My serigraphs and my paintings go to separate dealers.

(Woman)   How do you handle the expense and difficulty of framing?

(Genn)   If you work in oils or acrylics, it's better to get the dealer to do the framing. It should be your object to manoeuvre the dealer into framing. There are several reasons for this. Frames don't travel well, they are heavy and expensive to ship, and they get damaged. They are often more difficult to repair than paintings. If you are sending frames across international borders you may have the additional problem of excise duty, which generally doesn't apply to the art itself.

Secondly, and most importantly, different countries, even different cities, have their own taste in frames, and while, in your opinion, your work may not look as good in their regional frames, it is more likely to find a home.

I recommend that you ask your dealer to do the framing, and then he can choose the appropriate style for his area, make the profit, and he can control the markup on the frames. There is another good reason for this. Variations in pricing from city to city, which inevitably take place, can be attributed to the framing. Supply the paintings in standard sizes, as this allows the dealer to switch the frames from painting to painting and from artist to artist. When the dealers really take a look at the matter, they find it is best for them to supply the frames.

Framing is more of a problem with watercolours and pastels. They don't come in and out of frames as easily, and glass requires special treatment in shipping – taping, bubble-wrap, etc. You might

be advised to frame these yourself, and you might have to go to plex-
iglas if you ship.

(Woman) What are the standard frame sizes for oils and
acrylics?

(Genn) Starting with the small ones, in inches:

6 x 9
8 x 10
9 x 12
10 x 12
11 x 14
12 x 16
16 x 20
18 x 24
20 x 24
22 x 28
24 x 30
24 x 36
30 x 36
30 x 40
36 x 40
36 x 48

There are more.

(Woman) Have you ever heard of this? I was told by a gallery
that I could have a one man show if I was to pay six hundred dollars. Naturally I didn't go for it.

(Genn) I have. This is becoming common practice in some
parts of Europe and the United States. Some galleries have a user fee
and a very high commission rate. It's a holdup, of course. But you
have to look at the track record of the gallery in question. Does he
have a stellar mailing list with regular and current collectors – or is
he dependent on yours? Were previous artists satisfied? What sort of
promotion does the gallery provide? In London the gallery I chose
had its own fancy mailing list with lots of aristocracy, but for me they
were apparently busy that night.

(Woman) How do you protect the copyright on a work of
art?

(Genn)   You are automatically protected when you sign your work. It is your property, or the property of your heirs, to reproduce or do with what they will, until fifty years after your death. The work of art may have gone through several owners at this point – you still own the reproduction rights to it.

When the subject of copyright comes up at the primary sale of the painting you may wish to charge for it, or you may not. Sometimes, if they ask me, I give the copyright away.

Interestingly, if a painting is a commission, that is, someone other than a dealer has requested, specified and paid for the work – then the copyright rests with the commissioner.

If you want more information about these concerns I recommend *The Business of Art,* by Lee Caplan. Another good book, particularly for Canadian concerns, is *The Art World,* by Aaron Milrad. He is a valuable Toronto art-lawyer.

(Woman)   What is the normal commission fee for a gallery?

(Genn)   My price list reads 33 1/3%. This has been the traditional commission – one third to the gallery and two thirds to the artist. Many galleries these days ask for 40/60 or even 50/50. I have a couple of galleries who do an outstanding job and I reward them with 40/60. But if galleries are just average and they want to go to the higher rate I tell them they can do it, but they won't get many, or any, paintings. I have other places to send my work, and generally the dealer stays on track. I guess you have realized I run my galleries like a mutual fund. The important thing is that percentages are negotiable, and I think that if your paintings were selling like crazy you might get galleries to work for you for ten percent.

Let's not forget that galleries owners are in the front line, taking the bugs in their teeth. They must attend to and listen to customers. They have the often tiring job of creating a mystique around an artist whose ego may already be overextended. Galleries often have high overheads and many staff. Most dealers earn every nickel.

(Man)   Does the dealer charge you for the framing?

(Genn)   No. He puts it on top of the unframed list price of the painting, and charges the customer.

(Woman)   How do you go about shipping your work?

(Genn)   It's quite simple to move unframed paintings around the country. You gather them up from your studio, staple or tape them together so they won't shift around, and put them into a corrugated cardboard mirror-box, which you close down to the desired size and tape up. Mirror boxes are available through box manufacturers. They have the words 'mirror box' printed on the outside, and I think handlers are extra careful with them. Seven years bad luck, and all that.

You address the box and fill out a little waybill that the companies provide in advance. Then you phone a courier service – Purolator, Loomis, or United Parcel Service, or one of the many others, and they come by in a few hours and pick it up. In my studio we leave the box outside under the eaves so that it's really and truly gone and I can get on with other things. The next day the parcel arrives in another city. The shipping company sends us a bill. It's conventional for the artist to prepay to the dealer, and for the dealer to prepay if and when he sends something back to the artist.

Moving paintings around the world is a little more difficult. You may have to engage a broker, who may be expensive, tedious, and often inconvenient. So much for free trade.

(Woman)   What about wooden boxes for shipping?

(Genn)   In the old days when I used to ship framed paintings I took hours building wooden boxes. I guess you could say box building is a nice change. I used to value it as an avoidance activity for my main job in life.

(Woman)   Canvasses are bulky when travelling. How many do you take?

(Genn)   I take pre-gessoed sheets of canvas and when I get to Europe, or wherever, I staple them to standard-sized stretchers. I have the stretchers over there ahead of me on location because continental and most foreign stretchers are in centimeters. I paint my paintings in acrylic, then I take them off and roll them up in a newspaper and send them by newspaper post to my dealers. When they reach the dealer, he has the canvases put onto stretchers.

(Woman)   What about insurance when you ship?

(Genn)   I don't bother. It's a bit of a hassle. I've never lost a package in shipping. Once in a while things get stolen from gal-

leries, and the loss is covered by the galleries' insurance. I consider it more of an honor to have them properly stolen. I'd rather have my paintings stolen than my ideas. If I give my ideas away that's another matter.

We'll finish this hour by drawing your attention to an idea that has valuable motivational implications. It's called Creation Therapy.

Creation Therapy says that the essential mode of the universe is the act of creation. For example, stars, nebulae and solar systems have been creating themselves throughout time. They are in the process of being created at this very moment, and they will continue to be created in the future. Life itself is constantly in a process of creation and re-creation.

Creation is a wonder that no one fully understands. Attempts by philosophers, religionists, and even scientists, seem too pat to fully explain the miracle of creation. But it is impossible to escape the idea that it is central to the flow of the universe. Following this logic it would seem that in order to be fully realized as human beings we might fill our time with some form of creation. If we do this we are better able to join in the great stream, and thus, according to Creation Therapy theory, we are more fulfilled.

I like this idea. Long ago I learned I could turn an unhappy day into a happy one by painting a couple of reasonable paintings. I have often heard artists say: "I am only happy when I am at work." Or, "When I create I get a sense of my own self worth." Or, "When I create I feel I am making a contribution."

There is a possibility that compulsive creators have a purchase on life – an enriched being – one that is denied the average person. These creators may experience greater joys, and greater sadness, and are thus more in touch with the human condition and the bitter-sweet nature and irony of the universe. What more could an artist want?

Non-productivity, whether because of laziness, fear, or inability, is static. Creativity is dynamic, it asserts life, frees the human spirit, conquers mental lassitude and perhaps even illness, and makes real the outrageous potential of the universal imagination.

Hour 5

Women as Artists

(Genn) I overheard a woman say that she didn't think a woman's signature on a painting was as good as a man's. A few years ago the Grumbacher people did a study to find out how many artists there were in North America. They determined that there were seven and one half million people on this continent who had paints and called themselves artists. And seven million of them were women. Most of the artists that we all know about are men. And most of the prominent artists who apparently do great things are men. Why?

(Woman) Because it is a male dominated world.

(Woman) Men get away with murder.

(Woman) You fell into the trap yourself, Robert, when you saw that nice painting of Roslyn's, and you said it looked like one a man might have done. 'Strong masculine strokes,' you said.

(Genn) I meant it had bravura, sorry. Freudian slip.

(Woman) You can't win if you are a woman.

(Woman) The art business-world sees women as dabblers and hobbyists who may at any time go off and have a baby. Whereas a man is taken seriously right from the start.

(Woman) It's difficult if not impossible for a woman to work at home.

(Woman) I work at home and it works very well.

(Genn) The home can be the ideal workplace. Millions of frazzled commuters would love to work at home. There's no place like home.

(*Woman*)   We're so used to looking after our husbands, or the kids, or answering the phone, that we let the home intrude and we can't get to work. If we could get out of there we could just forget the responsibilities we have at home.

(*Genn*)   There is a lady in this seminar whose circumstances I am familiar with. All of her children have grown up and flown the coop, the coop is paid for and full of labour-saving devices so she doesn't drudge any more. Her husband is a born-again fisherman, and during the season he doesn't need his dinner for weeks at a time. She has a life of leisure, good fortune, and freedom.

(*Man*)   What we are trying to figure out is with seven million potential female artists out there, why don't more of them become succesful and even famous.

(*Genn*)   Thank you for putting us back on track. I've got a vested interest in this. I want to help people improve and become more successful, and in most cases the people I'm seeing in my practice as an 'art-psychiatrist' are women.

(*Man*)   Perhaps it is because men still control most of the disposable income.

(*Genn*)   Do you think men will buy men's art before they will buy the art of a woman?

(*Man*)   They probably are attracted to masculine type things.

(*Man*)   I'm more attracted to feminine type things.

(*Man*)   But then you are an artist. The guy who's got the money is probably a left-brainer and he's looking at it more as an investment. Male artists are safer, because of historical precedent.

(*Genn*)   You have a good point. Lawyers, doctors, and accountants represent a high percentage of collectors, and the percentage of women in those professions grows every year. In my experience, in middle class yuppie homes it is often the woman who makes art decisions. At least she sets it up for her husband's participation. Things have been changing over the last few years. It is getting to be more of a level playing field for women, for both the kicker and the receiver.

(*Woman*)   Women artists have been known to sign their

names in such a way as to be 'passed off' as men.

(Man)   Ridiculous.

(Woman)   This is a time when women are emerging. They are not staying submissive and at home. But we haven't quite gained the power to stand by our work in the way men, from childhood, have always been encouraged to do.

(Genn)   I would like to follow up on that. Perhaps women have always had the power. I feel women lack 'strategy.' Women often get credit for being strategic, but they are not generally strategic, compared to men. Furthermore, I feel that successful artists, whether male or female, are somewhat androgynous, that is, the classy guys have a certain amount of femininity, and the classy women have a degree of masculinity. In the males they have sensitivity, attention to detail, patience – all traditional female virtues. Conversely, the female has strategy, planning, and career orientation. Both must bring talent and dedication to bear. Androgyny has nothing to do with homosexuality.

(Man)   I feel art is an ideal vocation for women because the barriers are more easily broken down. These days women seem to want to break into the armed forces. I'm not trying to keep women out of the armed forces, but it seems to me that art is a natural vocation for women.

(Woman)   Here's a quote from Charlotte Whitton: "Whatever women do, they must do twice as well as men to be thought half as good. Luckily, it's not difficult."

(Man)   One of the effective ways to improve is to have a mentor. Men, because of their competitive nature, do not mentor other men as well as they do women. Because there is power involved, men mentor women. Also, because of their gregarious and mutually supportive nature, women mentor women.

(Man)   From what appears in art shows, I would say that women's paintings generally seem to be weaker and less vigorous than men's.

(Genn)   I'm glad the day is ending on a pleasant note.

(Woman)   Women do all the cooking, but all the famous

cooks are men.

(*Man*)   Women should be creative wonders. If they have been homemakers they were constantly required to come up with interesting and varied cooking. Kitchen artistry should be good training.

(*Woman*)   Why should women have to paint like men just to get accepted?

(*Genn*)   They don't. Galleries are not dominated by men any more. Collectors, decorators, interior designers, curators, and museum directors are not concerned with gender. Furthermore, many of the finest and most successful and courageous people in the arts are women.

(*Woman*)   The world has such a crumby perception of women.

(*Woman*)   Berthe Morisot and Mary Cassatt are now recognized among the greatest impressionists.

(*Woman*)   What about Georgia O'Keefe?

(*Man*)   She was the exception that proves the rule.

(*Woman*)   I think we women are discouraged. We need to emphasize our excellent role models.

(*Genn*)   I want to encourage you in that.

(*Woman*)   I feel strongly that a lot of women in my generation were led to believe that they would find a man who would earn the income, and I have come into a time when I realize that I have an equal right to the responsibility and the benefit, but I don't think I own the power. It wasn't integrated into my system. I am always fighting that. What's the use? I probably won't make it anyway. But I feel if I pass through life with a man, his success will be enough for us both. Female dependency goes back thousands of years.

(*Woman*)   Our mothers taught us that we weren't allowed to play until the ironing was done. And it's hard to get out of that way of thinking.

(*Genn*)   A man was walking by a circus, and he saw an elephant tied up with a very light rope fastened to a small spike in the ground. The elephant could easily get away, he thought, so he told the trainer. The trainer said that when the elephants are young they are very strong, so they tie them with a heavy chain anchored in concrete. The baby elephants tug and pull on the chain, trying to get away. But they soon realize that they can't escape, and after that anything can be used to tie up an elephant and keep it in its place.

(Woman)   I deplore the lack of 'free mind time.' You can find the time to be free of your drudgery, but your mind won't settle down from what it has to do. I am bothered by the fragmentation of my day.

(Genn)   That bothers me too. My wife and I figured out that we each drove our kids to the Yamaha School of Music 400 times. Each. All of us, men and women alike, have personal impedimenta in our lives. Michaelangelo had personal problems, financial problems, scaffolding problems, deadline problems. Rubens had to meet a big payroll every week.

A few years ago I did a workshop in Washington State, and the artists were all elderly women. One of them said to me that she had taken up painting when her husband died. As I went my rounds, I found most of them didn't have husbands. I began to wonder where all of the husbands had gone. I concluded they were dead of stress, or overwork, or underutilization.

What I would like to know is if women have it so bad why are the cruise-ships full of widows looking for replacements?

(Woman)   Mr. Genn, you have an assistant now to do all of your running around.

(Genn)   So did Georgia O'Keefe. A cute young guy.

(Woman)   Georgia's husband told her not to have children because it would dissipate her creative energy.

(Man)   It's the same for men. It really dissipates your energy.

(Woman)   Are men necessary?

(Genn)   Some of you have seen my book, *In Praise of Painting.* I have often thought of writing one called 'In Praise of Women.' I have a feeling that as well as being the gentler, fairer sex, they might also be the more truthful, caring, loving, and creative. When I look at the mess that male dominated governments

have made of the world, it makes me think that anyone could be elected provided that person was female. It's worth a try. I don't think as many sons would go to war if mothers were running the world. Perhaps we are coming to the end of a great male epoch. Men have been intrinsically stodgy and conservative and unimaginative. Look at the clothes they wear. It's time for women to have a kick at the can.

In 1988 I wrote a little book called *The Dreamway,* which featured a woman as oracle. It was about a bag-lady who carried around in her head all of the wisdom of the ages. I have been accused of being too zealous about the capacity and potential of women. Perhaps I will modify my views when I get older.

(Man)   Men probably have just as many extra jobs as women.

(Woman)   I think it is important for women to think about establishing themselves before taking on obligations. Then it is easier to set up parameters for time and energy. The whole concept of marriage is suspect in my opinion.

(Genn)   Last week I was in Paris and I went to the Montparnasse Cemetery and sat for a few minutes on the grave of Simone de Beauvoir. She's buried with Jean-Paul Sartre, and even though they were never married they put her on top of him, so now they can 'exist' together. *The Second Sex,* by de Beauvoir, is full of brilliant and often amusing insights. She says the only difference between marriage and prostitution is the length of the contract. She has a chapter on the independent woman, and she deals with the lack of symmetry in relationships.

(Woman)   When a man takes the kids to music, that's a plus for him. But women are expected to do that. A woman feels guilty if she doesn't.

(Man)   Some of you are talking as if you have a disability. I think what Genn is saying is that there can be a fortuitous transition from your home to your studio, and that you can do it. With regard to women not making it, a high percentage of the people I admire in the arts are women.

(Woman)   There is historical precedent, however. We know that men are in charge, and women have had a specific role to play,

and women who have struck out through the years of history have had a tough road. We know this from music, and literature, and art. But we are now more open about it, and more and more women are wanting to do things. And I think we are getting to the point in female development where we have to accept the fact that we have the choice. We don't necessarily have to do the things expected of us anymore. It isn't easy, because if you have been raised, as women in my generation were, to believe that if you painted as well as the man beside you, you didn't let him know, because that would damage his ego. It might even affect your social position. I feel it's important that we know we have the right to choose, and that our children have the right too. We must be accountable for what we do. We choose between artistic production and apple pie. We have to decide which is the more important to us.

(*Man*)   An apple pie would go down good right now.

(*Genn*)   I think women have to work harder to limit their feelings of guilt. I feel you have to ask yourself, this day, or this hour, or this minute, to start organizing yourself in a more strategic way.

Organize your space. You should not paint at the kitchen table, confusing your work with your domesticity. A room in the basement or garage can generally be found. If you really want to paint, you will find a better place. Men who want to paint will set up in the strangest places, and you might have to do likewise. You must have a private sanctuary into which you can disappear.

Secondly, you should heighten your sensitivity to time. An hour is a golden period. A lot can happen in an hour. Our school days were broken up into bite-sized segments of an hour, or sometimes forty minutes. The bell rang us in and out, with recesses between. It's a time honoured and valuable concept.

No one is going to hand you an organizational chart. You have to hand it to yourself. You have to say, 'This hour is mine to paint, the next hour is the pie hour, then it's back to paint.' You might consider rewarding yourself with an hour of painting for an hour of domesticity, or vice versa. Try bringing a day-planner or an organizer into your life for a while. This way you can keep an eye on your backsliding and monitor your progress. Respect space. Respect time.

(*Woman*)   Many women have time for TV.

(Genn)   The statistics are not pleasant. Women are up to twenty-eight hours of TV a week in Canada and the United States. Almost eight hours more than men. With the exception of some specially designated programs women are tending to watch practically anything. Researchers have suggested that many women watch because they have nothing better to do.

There is a price to pay for TV; it gives no joy to the hands.

(Woman)   We must ask ourselves what it is that causes us to procrastinate. Some of us will do anything not to go to work.

(Genn)   The reason can be fear of failure, but it might also be fear of success. What are they going to do when success arrives, how are they going to handle their husband and their money? Fear promotes mediocre effort.

(Woman)   When my husband asks me to iron his pants, I will tell him to iron them himself.

(Genn)   What you can do with your husband is strategic training over a period of time. You will eventually help him to accept what you are, but the change will have been gradual enough that he won't really notice. The women I've counselled to do this have found that their husbands love them even more than before, they find them more interesting, more accomplished, and capable of an exciting life of their own. And when kudos and success arrive, the husbands want to share the glory.

(Woman)   Fat chance.

(Woman)   Do you think women see things differently than men?

(Genn)   I don't see why not. Researchers at Stanford University have been releasing studies of male-female differences, some of which relate to creativity. Men make good experts, they found, but women have an inherent superiority when it comes to seeing the gestalt, or the big picture. Males tend to be more interested in objects than in people, even though they are generally more curious. Females are more attentive and have better verbal skills. Frequently the female surpasses the male in tasks involving manual dexterity, fine coordination, and rapid choice. Psychologists have determined that the hemispheres of the female brain interact earlier

than in males. This early maturity in women may in some cases arrest the child within them, distancing them from it. It has been my experience that when creative women manifest their child, they do it in spades.

Women have better skin sensitivity than males, they hear better, have a more highly developed sense of taste, and they carry a tune better than males. There is no reason to think they don't see things differently.

(Woman) Women operate with more highly sensitive emotions than men. They are more affected by those emotions. I think women have to feel good in order to do good, as compared to men who are more ego-based and have to do good in order to feel good.

(Woman) I think women are more conscious of their biorhythms than men are, and this can be taken advantage of in pursuing their creative interests. Also, productivity ebbs and flows during the female monthly cycle.

(Genn) How many women here feel they do more work or are more creative in the week after their periods? (2)

In the week before? (7)

Don't notice any difference, or don't know? (3)

(Woman) When I am working at my best I work with bursts of magical energy and I feel that I stretch myself beyond normal physical limitations. This can change in the next week or day and my work can become slow, methodical and even boring. Sometimes I find it necessary to stop for a complete rest. I allow myself this time to rest and I paint paintings in my head. Sometimes these periods are so long that I fear I will never paint again, or when I do I will have forgotten how.

(Woman) With regard to male and female expectations I often think of the toys that are produced for boys and girls. Boys have building materials. Girls have dolls. Childrens' toys mold their future.

(Woman) Is it possible for anyone, male or female, to oppose their unfortunate upbringing, break out of their molds, and affirm themselves into positive results?

(Genn)   A few years ago I devised a little affirmation that I have typed out and enlarged on the photo-copier, and given to many painters. Some of them think it helps.

I am a creator
I make things
I love what I do
I love myself
I rest and look ahead
I examine my plans
I visualize my projects
I work with joy
I take risks
I frequently win
I add my winnings to my winnings
I have a clear conscience, I am stimulated, I am constantly moving forward, and I am accountable.

What this last idea means is that you simply do not allow yourself to become guilty, bored, paralysed, or victimized.

Did you notice that remark a minute ago, about males being the more curious? We all dislike generalizations, but they sometimes give us a clue as to how we might improve. The story I'm going to tell happens to be about a man, but I think it might be useful for anyone.

I met a bright fellow who taught film appreciation and film history in a university. When I suggested that we work together making a film he exhibited what I thought was an extraordinary desire not to take part in any such thing. He would break out in a sweat whenever I mentioned the subject. One day I phoned his wife when he wasn't home and asked if I could come over. To his home I took my 16mm Bolex with a Vario-Switar zoom lens, fader, and various other accessories. I set it up on my professional tripod in the middle of his living room, and asked his wife to keep me informed as to what might happen.

The next day she phoned to say he had seen it there and asked her to phone and get me to come and pick it up. I didn't.

A few days later she phoned and very quietly told me that he had his hands on the camera and was looking through the lens. Several days later she phoned to say he had his hands on it all the time and was panning, zooming and dissolving. He had even built a dolly for it and was practicing tracking shots.

I knew it was just a matter of time. In a while he phoned to say that we should do something about his idea for a co-project. We made his first movie the next weekend.

My point is that one has to get their 'hands on' in order to develop. As M.P. Follett says in *Creative Experience*, "Concepts can never be presented to me merely, they must be knitted into the structure of my being, and this can only be done through my own activity."

While the story I have told is about a man, I think it points to a condition found in many women. A man is more likely to say, "I wonder how this will turn out?" whereas a woman is likely to say, "This is how I want it to turn out."

I can see that some of you women disagree with me.

Perhaps I could draw your attention to two books.

The first is *What We May Be,* by Piero Ferrucci. It's a companion for a person who is working on psychological or spiritual growth. It advocates psychosynthesis, which is a transformation technique developed by the Italian psychologist Roberto Assagioli. There are parts of this book which are valuable for people like us. Ferrucci deals with the imagination and esthetics. The human psyche, he says, no matter how damaged or stubborn, is infinitely moldable and has unlimited possibilities.

The second book is *The Possible Human,* by Jean Houston. Some of you may be familiar with her material. This is a course in building the physical, mental, and creative abilities. She has a fairly comprehensive theory and program for conscious creativity, and she talks a lot about strategies used by successful artists and others. I like her ideas on the epiphany of the moment. She also goes into right brain and left brain, and multitracking.

(Woman)   What's epiphany and multitracking?

(Genn)   An epiphany is the sudden illumination, or breakthrough, or vision that we experience from time to time. Multitracking means training your mind to work on many problems simultaneously. Accessing your subconscious mind to come up with solutions and new ideas while you are busy on other projects.

I'd like to tell you a little story about women and men. I was instructing a group on Saltspring Island and Sara and James, my twins, were along with me. They were about eight years old. One of the artists I was supposed to be instructing was a woman by the name of Loretta. She was having a terrible time settling down. She told me that she thought that making little easel paintings was a bore, and that she wanted to do something important. She wanted to do her work right on the landscape itself. She had an idea how she could do it but she lacked the courage. I agreed to help her and we went together and bought buckets of paint, and giant brushes, and we borrowed a pick and a shovel. Loretta proceeded to dig a trench down the beach and out across the sand at low tide. On the other side of the bay she painted two stripes up the beach and finished it off with a big bull's-eye on a boulder. The other artists went about their business. Sara and James and I helped Loretta from time to time; it was quite satisfying to paint right on the beach-rocks. A lot of curious and even hostile neighbors who owned beach-front properties came down to see what was happening. Loretta was careful to tell everyone that the paint was biodegradable and nothing would be harmed, but I did see a few oddly coloured crabs running around.

As the sun went down and the tide came in to erase her effort Loretta had a chance to explain herself, and she admitted to the group that it was easier than she had thought, that it was somehow satisfying and that she was glad she did it. I was surprised to hear her say she would try to paint a skillful easel painting the next day.

The kids and I got into the station wagon to go back to the hotel and I asked them what they thought of the whole thing. Sara said, "Loretta is a very nice lady, she didn't hurt anything, and what she did was fun."

I asked James what he thought and he said, "Lock 'er up."

There is a method which is open to women to get a grasp and understanding of their potential and power. It is through the characteristics of the mythical goddesses. The main ones are Athena, Aphrodite, Persephone, Artemis, Demeter, and Hera.

Athena: education, career, competitor, intellectual.

Aphrodite: sexual, sensual, beauty, passion, patroness.

Persephone: visions, dreams, healing, psychic power.

Artemis: adventuress, huntress, shamaness, wild.

Demeter: earth mother, fertility, nurture.

Hera: tradition, marriage, partner, empress.

What you do is examine those goddesses dominant within yourself. As your life unfolds you may find your goddesses changing along with it. Traditional Hera may have flowered into sensual Aphrodite. Fertile mother Demeter may be overtaken by a careering Athena. With an understanding of the goddesses within, you are better able to live and flow in your true nature. Two excellent books on the subject are *The Goddess Within,* by Jennifer and Roger Woolger, and *Goddesses in Everywoman,* by Jean Shinoda.

The idea behind all of this, for men as well as women, is not just survival, but 'thrival.'

Our homework tonight is to look over the key words; and if you wish you may prepare some remarks, thoughts, or observations. You are a great group, full of energy, and a lot of fun. Some of you gentlemen received a few scratches in the donnybrook. I hope you can explain everything to your wives.

Hour 6

Nuts and Bolts

(Genn)   Hello. Good Morning. Thank you for joining us. Emerson said, "No one expects the days to be gods." What shall we do today?

(Woman)   Nuts and bolts.

(Genn)   Remember when I said at the beginning that this wasn't going to be a workshop on how to paint? But we did seem to agree that the artist, to be effective, and to get into the "joy mode" – had to be on a first name basis with his materials. So let's take this hour to look at some of the details of our craft; techniques, materials, methods, media, systems.

(Woman)   I really enjoy looking at your paintings, Robert. Your colours are wonderful, and there is consistency in style.

(Genn)   I suppose one's style is somewhat automatic. There is perhaps something that an artist can't control that comes with time.

(Man)   What do you put on your acrylic paintings to give them the gloss?

(Genn)   Acrylic polymer emulsion varnish gloss. I cut the varnish about fifty-fifty with water. I lay the canvas on the floor and pour a generous amount onto the painting. Then I brush it out in all directions, from time to time looking at it against the light to see if there are any holidays. Then I tip the canvas up and let the excess run off back into the bottle. When it is down to a drip I put the canvas back onto the floor, and give it a check for doggy-hairs and things like that.

This varnishing gives a moderate shine and evens out the duller areas. If you want more shine you wait half an hour until the first coat is dry and repeat the process. It has the effect of sealing the painting with a perfectly clear protective coat from which fly-specks and grime can be removed over the years with a washcloth.

It's important to note that you can't work again on top of the varnish. The molecules that hold the paint to paint will be isolated from each other by the varnish which is a different molecule, and the retouching can be easily wiped away. There is a small expensive bottle of acrylic varnish remover which you can buy if you want to go back and work on a painting. I use ordinary household ammonia of the sudsy variety to clean off the final varnish if I want to touch up. I take the painting outside where the fumes are not as offensive, and I spread the ammonia on with a cloth and then wash it all off with a hose. The painting stays perfectly safe and the touch-up work adheres to the dry paint.

Oils require an oil-based final picture varnish. I generally use retouch varnish in a spray can. If used sparingly I don't think the work has to be totally dry. Ideally, it is a good idea to wait a couple of weeks before varnishing an oil painting. Another product goes under the name of 'Final Picture Varnish,' and is generally applied with a brush. Oil-based final picture varnish can be removed with turpentine or turpentine substitute or solvent. On older paintings toluene or toluol is sometimes used.

(Woman)   Do you prefer oils or acrylics?

(Genn)   They both have their beauties and their disadvantages. I like to say what you lose on the straights you make up on the corners. For those that haven't tried acrylics I recommend you explore them. They don't have the juicy, buttery quality which is so appealing in oils, but they have other qualities, not the least of which is the speed of drying. Some people feel they dry too fast, particularly when you are trying to work outdoors in the sunlight. After you become proficient with them you will probably feel that they are not drying fast enough.

Acrylics have the ability to hold their colour. Oils I painted thirty years ago are showing signs of linseed oil darkening, but acrylics of the same age look to me as they did on the day they were painted.

(Woman)   What brand of acrylics do you use?

(Genn)   I like to use the most popular brand in whatever country I'm in. They are likely to be the freshest in the art shops, and it is interesting to explore their various nuances. I have a recurring fantasy that some day I will walk into some foreign art shop and there will be a totally new colour.

Incidentally, formulas in acrylic resins vary from brand to brand and may not always bind with each other. I don't think it's a good idea to mix brand with brand.

(Woman)   Do you have a problem with acrylics darkening as they dry?

(Genn)   You get used to it and you learn to make automatic adjustments.

(Woman)   Are there any other reasons for using acrylics?

(Genn)   There is one reason above all others that I made a general change into acrylics. Health. About 1984 I read a book called *Artist Beware* by Michael McCann, which frightened me with the volatile solvents in oils. The book deals with the hazards and precautions in working with art and craft materials. I began to think I might be inhaling myself to an early death. I now think acrylics are safer. It is important of course not to put paint of any kind into your mouth, and I think it is poor form to smoke while painting. This goes for acrylics too, and I am not sure but I think using a hair-dryer to dry acrylics releases toxic gasses from the medium. I don't think there is as much of a problem with watercolour.

I knew a relatively young artist who used a lot of hydrocarbon spray-cans, and who painted in oils in a confined, unventilated space, and he has gone to the big studio in the sky. I didn't want to join him. People were coming into my studio and saying the atmosphere was really thick, and I wasn't noticing it, so I made my decision to move to water.

(Woman)   I want to ask some questions about colour. How do you achieve your greys?

(Genn)   I generally mix opposites on the colour-wheel, say blue and orange until it is really neutral, then I add a bit of black and white. Sometimes I start with white and noodle in some colours. I

try to avoid those pasty whitish greys. I practically never use black and white alone.

Some artists whom I admire spend a lot of time pre-mixing their colours on their palettes, and I think this is probably the best way. I mix each as I need it, and I think it slows me down a bit, but more importantly it is likely to get my painting out of whack, and some effort has to be made to pull it together afterward.

In the last few years I have been taking little yogurt cups, the ones with lids, and pre-mixing colours in quantity. I mark the cup with a number or put a smear on the lid. The colours don't dry out, and they're very handy because you know what the colour will do and you can go from painting to painting with them. We consume a lot of yogurt at our house.

(Woman)   Do you find acrylics sometimes develop a mold?

(Genn)   Yes, and I don't know the cause or the antidote. They sometimes smell bad too. When this happens I throw them out.

(Man)   You have a kind of vibrating grayish iridescent sheen in some of your paintings. How do you get that?

(Genn)   I think you might be referring to the "Nelson Tri-Hue System." Some of you may have attended some of Dick Nelson's workshops. He is a watercolour artist and colour theorist who lives in Hawaii. The system involves using the three primary colours similar to those used by commercial printers: process yellow, magenta, and cyan. I like to tell Dick that I don't use the 'full-Nelson' system, but rather a 'half-Nelson.' He is annoyed at me for not being pure. I like interplaying the warp and woof of his ideas with my own ideas. He doesn't believe in using white, for example. But in an opaque system, such as acrylic or oils, I feel you have to use white. You need white for contrapuntal effects. Dick Nelson's pure idea works best in transparent watercolour.

It's a great learning experience. I'll give you the pigments for it. First in watercolour:

(Winsor and Newton)
Cadmium lemon
Alizarin crimson
Winsor blue

(Grumbacher)
Lemon yellow
Thalo crimson
Thalo blue

If you take these three colours and layer them on top of one another with drying between, you can theoretically and essentially achieve any colour.

In most brands of acrylics the pigments you need are:

Hansa yellow light
Rose-red
Pthalo blue

Here's how I perform a 'half-Nelson.' Working generally on a light grey-toned ground or imprimatura, I set up my painting in a rough way by laying in the main areas. Then I take the painting and lay it on the floor, and with a fan brush I criss-cross in the yellow. It is important to get the yellow down first because it is the lightest and also the most opaque. I am careful not to cover everything. When that is dry, I criss-cross it with the red, and then again with the blue. The degree of transparency of the colours depends on how dark I want it to go. When all is dry it gives the impression of a sort of woven plaid with bits of bright colour here and there. The general tone-value has been brought lower and from a distance it appears to be quite grey. Up close it is dancing with colour. Then I take the painting back to the easel and put in various tones, some in opaque scumble, and some in transparent washes. It sounds laborious, but really it is very fast and a lot of fun. Sometimes, and this is the part where Dick could shoot me, I glaze the whole thing with burnt sienna or black, or one of several other colours. I spread the whole glaze on with a rag in the areas where I want it, and keep wiping it off until the desired degree of darkness of the glaze is established. One of the golden qualities of acrylics is that you can glaze during the painting event. You don't have to wait for days as you do in oils.

With this system I had a good period which resulted in a series of Brittany paintings and the ones I did of my daughter Sara in a striped dress. These works really glow, and have an excitement to their surfaces. After a while, however, my work started to deteriorate, and the colours became garish and out of control. I knew there was something wrong, and I just couldn't put my finger on what it was. I was like a person with diabetes who didn't know it. I just couldn't get to the root of the problem.

Then one day it came to me. I've always felt a kinship with Claude Monet. I felt him to be a fellow traveller, and I've visited his studio at Giverny. His impressionist palette interested me. I was reading about his methods, and he was saying, "Black is the queen of colours." I discovered Renoir felt the same way. This shook me up. I realized that there is a fourth colour in the printers' palette that Dick had left out – black.

Right away I was able to move into a new period. I began toning down my paintings with black glazes, and popping in my lights which now came alive as never before. Sometimes the glazes were extremely weak, but they gave my work a new solidity.

(Man)   What is a glaze?

(Genn)   A glaze is a transparent overpainted wash, usually of a darker colour than what lies under it. A scumble is an opaque overpainting, usually of a lighter colour. It is possible to combine the two. Effective foggy moods can be produced with a semi-opaque white glaze. If you look at darker parts of paintings done in this way, you will see tiny granules of white which have the effect of raising the tone value.

If you wish to glaze in oils you can try *Shiva Signature Permasols*. These are transparent oils, including transparent white; they are good for adding color to shadows, and making water look wet and translucent.

(Man)   Have you tried alkyds? They seem to me to be the ideal compromise; fast drying and oil-based.

(Genn)   Alkyd resins are durable, flexible as acrylics, and they don't yellow. I experimented for a while and found them to be honey-like and syrupy, more like industrial paint. There is nothing wrong with the colours. It is the medium that bothers me. It's a personal thing.

(Woman)   What's wrong with linseed oil?

(Genn)   While it's the traditional and time honored oil medium, it is probably the worst. It yellows and darkens with age, especially when paintings are kept in a darkened area. You can prove this to yourself by laying a coin on an older painting and leaving it out in the sun for a day. Linseed oil as a medium can oxidize, wrinkle up, or crack if you don't use it right. Furthermore, linseed oil affects some pigments differently and tends to alter colour with time. All the traditional drying oils force you to work fat over lean, especially if you would like to see your work last a few centuries. I am told that much of what is labeled linseed oil doesn't come from flax anymore, but from sunflower, which is supposed to be not as subject to darkening.

(*Man*)   What kind of brushes do you use for acrylics?

(*Genn*)   I don't use the synthetic ones made especially for acrylics. I use four main brushes. Three oil and one watercolour.

Large fan brush.
Medium sharp bristle, say No.12
Smallish sharp bristle, say No.6
Medium sable, say No.6

These are the ones I would take to a desert island. Brushes are great fun; and if you include the oriental ones they come in hundreds of styles. The brushes that work best for me in acrylics are sharps, that is, the shorter of the two standard square ended bristles. I don't use filberts or rounds; my older brushes seem to get that way anyway. You have heard about the fellow who was a bit of a magician – he could walk down the street and turn into a tavern. I turn into a brush store. When I was in Paris last week I bought some beauties with really long handles that give a terrific sense of power and elan. I had to cut the handles in half in order to get them into the suitcase, and then I glued them back together at 3 A.M. when I returned to my studio.

In watercolour it's good to have a wide selection at hand as effects and variety are more frequently brush-related. My watercolor range includes large and small sables, fan brush, one-inch flat sable, sumi, fat goat-hair, various sponges, air brush. Instruments for removing colour include sticks, plastic brush protectors, rags, blotters, razor blades.

It's fun to use lots of different brushes when you are in a speculative mood. I make myself choose brushes that are a little bit larger than I need. Fan brushes were originally designed for portraiture, and for softening and fuzzing areas in oil. But they are wonderful for trees, grasses, and other effects. You can push against them and get some interesting results. I use them for softening edges and large areas, and I use them for the final varnish.

As a general rule I try to avoid using the sable, except for signing my name.

The brush is not as important as the person behind it. One time I was in a park doing a painting in the boot of my old Bentley. A man came by and watched me. He was very quiet, but his nose got closer and closer to my work. Finally he said, "That is a fantastic brush."

(Woman)   Do you use a gel or a medium in your acrylics?

(Genn)   A little. The medium is an additional binder. I use some medium in my glazes to make sure they stay put. I add a bit of medium when I am making up those little yogurt cups. Sometimes gel is useful for impasto passages, and generally adding body to the paint. Valuable effects can be made by scraping it away. The gel generally comes in a tube and the medium in a plastic bottle. They are the same thing, except that the gel is thicker than the medium.

(Woman)   I am very concerned with sinking-in in my work. Some areas are dull and others shiny.

(Genn)   A lot of sinking-in problems start with poor priming. Even though you have purchased a primed canvas, I recommend that you prime it again. I practically always work on a toned ground. Sometimes I put down a really bright ground, and fight against it, so to speak. Some colours tend to sink in more than others. Oxides absorb twice their weight in medium. Burnt umber, for example, sucks up a lot and goes dull. Use a little extra medium for the absorbant colours. Generally the final varnish will pull it together.

(Woman)   How do you prime your canvases?

(Genn)   With a roller. I do a couple of dozen at a time, and change the tone a bit so I have a variety of grounds. The best ground is gesso, with the acrylic colour added. I love to have a tone on the canvas, it gives the feeling that the painting is already started. I put it on fairly thinly, well diluted with water. Sometimes I put on two

coats. Some artists like the effect of gesso when put on stiffly with a brush. Some artists can't live without a pure white gesso.

(Man)   Where do you buy your art materials?

(Genn)   I believe in supporting the people in my community. The result is the few times I have run out of blue on a Sunday afternoon, I have been able to make a phone call and the shop owner will go down and open up for me. When it's getting near year-end I generally give her a large order. But I am always patronizing the local shop for this and that, if only to find out what's new.

(Man)   What do you look for in a brand of paint?

(Genn)   Freshness. Consistency. Strength. Some artists like it loose so that they can trail it out in longer, more elegant strokes. I generally like it short and stiff, so it sits up.

(Man)   I buy jars of white. How do you feel about jars of colour, as opposed to tubes?

(Genn)   Jars are for people who can remember to put on the lids. It is easy to set up a range with little jars, too, and I suppose if you were careful jars could be more economical. For some reason, perhaps tradition, I still like tubes.

(Woman)   How do you keep your paints wet overnight?

(Genn)   I generally don't. I squeeze out fresh in the morning. You can use the little wet-sheets like Rowney 'Stay-Wet' palette membrane and reservoir paper. Or you can give them a spray of water with an atomizer. Covering a wet palette with a low lid seems to work. You can put a little retarder around the paint and some saran-wrap over and it will last too. But I like to work on a fresh strip-palette.

(Man)   Do you ever use canvas-boards?

(Genn)   I did in my less palmy days. And I am sorry I did. They don't hold up too well. Certain bugs enjoy the glue in them, and if they get moist they can be trouble. Furthermore, they have the association of an amateur support. Nothing beats fresh springy canvas.

(Man)   Some of your work is on wooden panels. What do you use and how do you prepare them?

(Genn)   I use wooden panels for smaller sizes, generally 8x10 and 10x12. They are thin mahogany plywood which is sold in the lumber stores under the name of 'door-skin'. I have a carpenter cut up a few hundred for me at a time on a table saw. I prime them with 'glue size' made from Weld-Bond or other carpenters' glue. It is quite severely diluted with water so it penetrates the wood. I size the front and back and edges to prevent warping and the penetration of moisture between the layers. When dry the panel is sanded and a coat of transparent acrylic medium is applied, sometimes with a tint of some sort. I like to let the grain and some of the colour of the wood show and it becomes part of the painting. The little panels fit into a portable panel-box which holds a dozen or so. This makes them very handy, especially for location work.

Panel painting is a tradition. Artists such as John Constable and J.M.W. Turner sketched on basswood and mahogany. Tom Thompson and members of Canada's Group of Seven worked on wood. Colours sit up on wood when it's well prepared.

(Man)   What about masonite?

(Genn)   There is acid in tempered masonite which must be sealed off with a good primer or the work will severely yellow in time. If you must use masonite I recommend the untempered variety. Prime it well. At least twice. Untempered masonite is the lighter-coloured of the two; tempered is darker in tone and shinier.

(Woman)   Do you still gesso the backs of your canvas?

(Genn)   I forgot about that. I did for a short while, but I don't anymore. There is one painting group that I have been visiting every once in awhile for about twenty years, in which there is a woman who has written down everything that I have ever said. And it bothers me to go there now because she is constantly putting up her hand and saying, "But Mr. Genn, in 1974 you said.... etc." I love to change my mind.

(Woman)   Have you ever worked on a very dark toned ground?

(Genn)   Yes. Even black. It's like working on black velvet – do you remember black velvet? – you are constantly building up to light. Very dark imprimaturas must be isolated from the paint by a layer of medium or the later colours will tend to darken, especially

in oils. Interesting effects can be created with this method. The dark can be left as lines with patches of colours between. With a medium tone, say a 50% grey ground, you can go first to one side and then to the other: darker darks, lighter lights, darkest darks, lightest lights. It's a valuable system for building up forms, particularly in figurative work.

(Man)   Have you ever tried working with metallic colours?

(Genn)   Seldom. Last week in Paris I was with Joe Plaskett, and I found he has been using iridescent metallics in his newest pastels. He uses them as accents here and there and they're not offensive.

The iridescent pastels are suitable to Joe Plasketts' milieu. He lives in a fantastic sixteenth century post and beam walk-up that would fall into the street if it wasn't retained by iron bars. Every room is loaded with memorabilia: mirrors, candelabras, chandeliers, the props he uses in his work. The place is a movable feast. There are always interesting people coming and going at Joe's place. This year when I visited there was a man from the Smithsonian doing research on expatriate American and Canadian artists.

A couple of years ago I was exploring his home and I was in a bedroom looking at a four-poster bed that sagged down to the slanting floor. I became aware that a young woman wearing glitzy panties and bra was watching me quietly from the corner. I left the room and asked Joe who she was and he said, "Oh, that's Marie, she was a model for a while, and now I can't get up the nerve to ask her to move on."

(Man)   To what extent should I do colour-mixing for my work?

(Genn)   I think you would be well advised to get one of those Walter T. Foster books called *Colour Mixing* by Merlin Enabnit. He is somewhat of a colour wizard, and he tells you what you need to know to get rich, interesting colours. Opposites on the colour-wheel are his key.

(Woman)   How important do you think it is to have a set palette and stick to it?

(Genn)   I don't. I have gone from long palettes to short ones and back again. For a while I went minimalist and had a Churchill

cigar-box for my panel paintings. It would only hold four tubes, so I had cadmium red, ultramarine blue, cadmium yellow, and flake white. I wanted to be in a limited mode and explore the possibilities.

(Man) Do you keep a few frames around your studio to look at your paintings in?

(Genn) Yes. A frame gives a new perspective, prevents the artist from overworking the painting, and enhances the work. There are generally several framed paintings in various degrees of completeness on my secondary easel.

I put paintings temporarily into the frames with little snappy clips that are fast and handy. When the painting goes out to dealers the stretchers don't have any nail holes.

(Woman) What colours do you use?

(Genn) My acrylic palette changes from time to time. Right now I am working with a rather limited palette:

Hansa yellow light
Alizarin crimson
Pthalo blue
Cadmium orange
Cadmium red
Yellow ochre
Burnt sienna
Raw umber
Permanent green light
Mars black
Titanium white

One of the basic rules is not to add a colour to the palette after you have started on a painting. This is because a new element may upset the family of colours you have chosen. When I look at a subject I am going to work on, I sometimes decide in advance that I could use violet, or sap green, or something else, and I add that at the beginning.

I often notice when I watch beginners at work that they don't squeeze out enough colour. They have little miserable dabs of paint. I like to see an ample amount. Unless your style is very sparse, you should be able to mix generously. Just pretend you are wealthy, and you will be.

There are many excellent books which can help you to under-stand and trust materials. Perhaps the classic is *The Artist's Handbook of Materials and Techniques,* by Ralph Mayer. It's time honored, reliable and comprehensive.

Another good resource that is readily available is *Painting Materials,* by Rutherford Gettens and George Stout. It's exhaustive in mediums, adhesives, pigments, solvents, dilutents, supports, tools and equipment. It is highly detailed in the processes of manufacture and the history of materials.

A handsome and colourful book which I love is *Painting Methods of the Impressionists,* by Bernard Dunstan. He is a respectable British artist who has taken a close look at the painting processes of a few chosen and worthy painters; Manet, Pissarro, Degas, Cezanne, Cassatt, Vuillard, Bonnard, and others, and I feel secure in the correctness of his research and observations.

Our job has come a long way from the days when artists ground their own, or squeezed their pigments out of pigs' bladders. The chemistry of art is fun, and it is still valuable to know sources, characteristics, expectations, and long term permanence. I like to read these sorts of books on rainy days, or when I'm up in the air. They give a person respect for our business.

So much of what artists concern themselves with seems at first glance to be trifles. It's no mystery that we become particular about those trifles in our search for quality. In the words of Michaelangelo: "Trifles make perfection, and perfection is no trifle."

(Woman) Do you find that fluorescent lights affect your paintings adversely?

(Genn) Yes. I don't believe in them, even the ones with warm bulbs. I think paintings should be made under lighting of the same colour temperature as lights in galleries and homes. This generally means incandescents, although halogens and other cooler lights are now becoming popular. I have a 100 watt standard incandescent light on a movable neck mounted on my easel. Another good reason for using the warmer bulbs is that they more closely approximate the long light of the late afternoon, the favorite of artists like Sorolla who claimed to paint only in the 'magic hour.'

(Woman)   You seem to have a system for everything. Is this always good?

(Genn)   There are two main kinds of artists – those who have systems and those who do not. I find the system part of the joy. You may not. J.M.W. Turner was an artist without system. His non-system was a system.

Hour 7

Confession Time

(Genn)   Painting is a great adventure because it is a combination of spirit, chemistry, ideas, planning, talent, and hard work.

We're all friends here. There are no secrets we can't share. Who would like to address any of the key words?

(Woman)   I am an installation artist. I chose three words: originality, evolution and synergy.

For me originality is of primary importance. I have no interest in doing things that other people are doing. I want to do something unique. While I want to understand Rembrandt, I don't feel I would ever emulate him.

The evolution of my art reflects my evolution as a person. There have been dramatic developments in my life over the past few years. My art has reflected this and has changed along with it.

In the mathematics of synergy, one plus one is three, and two plus two is ten. We, as a group of individuals, have a greater power. I value the people in this group because I know there is a lot of talent and skill here, and I want to reach out to you to come to a show at my studio. Not that you would become customers, but you can give me the valuable feedback that I desire.

(Woman)   I decided to empty my mind and move my finger down the list, and where it stopped I circled the word. Then I tried to think of associations with the words I found. My words are: alone, which associated with madness and guilt; avoidance, associating failure and success; business, associating inventory and selling; ideas, associating copying, creativity and diversity; originality, associating sexual energy; and teaching, associating envy and learning.

This collection of words surprised me by summing up where I am right now and by featuring issues that are concerning me.

I would like to talk about originality and sexual energy. My personal concerns were coming out in my art. One of them was my sexual energy, particularly my femininity and my power as a woman. I found that no matter what subject I chose to paint it was coming out very sexual, very feminine, very genital. As many of you are aware there was a controversy over a show I had in December, and my paintings were taken down. I was called upon to defend myself in the newspapers and on TV, and as a result I feel I now own myself and who I am.

I was looking at wood grain, knotholes and that sort of thing, and this was getting into my work in a very feminine way, and people objected to it.

If you look at any wood grain it looks very male-female. One of my knotholes in particular looked too female. For me it was where I was at. It was sexualized in my identity, and it developed into a beautiful painting, nice colours, and subtle, I thought. My friends said there was a change in me, so I called the work 'Conception.' But the City Hall had it taken down. I had pieces in the show that were much more explicit than that one. One magazine called me, 'Canada's foremost genital artist.'

I finally had to decide to own my work and where I was coming from, and take responsibility for my actions. If my work offends people, then that is their prurient problem, not mine.

With regard to teaching, which I associated with envy and learning, I was an honors graduate from a highly respected art college. I feel I met with a great deal of male chauvinism while I was at that school. One of the instructors actually said, 'Go home and paint for a few years.' And in the next studio there was a male student who was recommended to galleries, and given other encouragement. When I asked why I wasn't helped in the same way, the instructor said, 'You will probably go home and have kids.'

Another time they brought in a famous artist from New York, and he saw and liked my work, but when he came to be introduced to me, the principal just belittled me in front of him.

(*Genn*) Congratulations for being so brave, and feeling your ideas deeply, and sharing them with us. You had times when you wondered whether you were doing the right thing, and other times you followed your intuition. It must have been a great catharsis to be able to do what you did.

There is a problem with artistic freedom and the presentation of what some people may call offensive material under the guise of fine art. In most cases I have taken Voltaire's view: "I disapprove of what you say, but I will defend to the death your right to say it." Here are some other, perhaps surprising, notions. Leonardo da Vinci said, "Art lives from constraints and dies from freedom." The cellist, Pablo Cassals, remarked, "We are not free to walk on our neighbors' toes."

The chauvinism-at-school situation is reported quite frequently. I was on the board at an art college for three years, and I wasn't a particularly popular member of that board. I could speak at length of the disservice that is done to echelons of young people who want to learn and get a fair shot. Students of both sexes with evident academic talent are sometimes belittled in front of others, but on the other hand so are students without great potential. It would seem that many instructors are angry, or bitter, or troubled.

(Woman) That problem is evident through the whole university system.

(Genn) It may be indigenous to the nature of schools and the methodology of teaching, but from this kind of adversity some of us are able to reap benefits. Art colleges, to their credit, introduce students to a wide range of disciplines, often have wonderful 'hands on' facilities, available studio space, and libraries specific to the subject.

(Man) How do you feel about art education at the university level?

(Genn) Art academics live in a world apart. I often feel it is as if they have all signed a declaration of agreed mutual bamboozlement. I recently attended a lecture by a guest artist in the Fine Arts Department at an Ontario university. The woman was a printmaker, film-maker, video-artist, painter, sculptress, and wood carver. Her slide show confirmed that she was incompetent in all media. The students were flummoxed. There was little one could learn from her. All the questions came from the other instructors, and added to the mystery.

(Woman) The word that I noticed in the list was depression. I am often depressed. Are you? What do you do?

(Genn)   Occasional depression is probably normal. The natural tendency is to fight it, or try to cheer up and not to let things get you down.

The way to beat it is to try to understand its source. We artists, the most privileged of humans, have nevertheless a great deal to be depressed about. The list is legion. Frequently, however, the condition can be narrowed to one area – our artistic inadequacy. We compete with all artists, alive and dead. We compete with the rare seeds of genius: Velasquez, Caravaggio, Renoir, Monet, Sargent, Sorolla. I try to be philosophic.

Here's a method for overcoming depression that works for me. When I feel a depression coming on, I drop what I'm doing, and I don't fight it. I go all the way and do a bit of crying if necessary. Then I go for a walk, alone, for at least half an hour. For some reason, the source of the depression can often be identified and made somewhat less important during a walk. I tend to count my blessings. I let my dog help me. I also try to look at beautiful things, or talk to people, or do some act of kindness.

I used to have depressions that lasted several weeks. Using the short walk method, I was able to limit my depression to a couple of hours. I think it often works because a fresh idea comes while walking. Ideas come on the hoof. Furthermore, if you let yourself go down harder you tend to come up faster.

I come back to the studio with spring in my step and I'm able to greet my work with a fresh eagerness. Sometimes there is the wondrous realization, "I can still paint." The art in itself is an expression of anti-depression and optimism. I may not be John Singer Sargent, but the feeling of brotherhood along his path is comforting.

A few years ago I heard a radio program about a man who had been interned in a Nazi prison camp during World War II. For three years he was subject to the most terrible humiliations. Death stalked the corridors. Frequently the Gestapo would select someone at random and take him out and shoot him. The man and his inmates lived in constant and desperate fear. The prisoners were regularly instructed to take off all their clothes and face a wall. Certain prisoners were brutally beaten in this position until they dropped. There was no medical help. The man who was narrating this story reported that one day while facing a wall awaiting a chance punishment, he thought to himself, "If I ever get out of this alive, please let me never be depressed about anything again."

Depression is a popular expression of how we feel, as well as a severe mental disorder, with a fuzzy line between. If anyone here is suffering prolonged and severe depression they should feel no stigma about seeking professional help.

A friend of mine suffered from occasional depressive moods, and one day he had a particularly bad one so he decided to check himself into the local mental institution. He went to the desk and stated his desire to commit. The woman gave him a neatly folded green coat and told him he would have to have a physical examination first and to go and wait in room 769. When he got to room 769 there were several depressed looking people already wearing green coats. More green coats moved up and down the halls. My friend thought that he could either put on – or not put on – the green coat. He put the coat on a chair and left the institution by the front door. A guard said to him, "Where are you going?"

"Out," he said, "I just dropped in."

The guard said "Okay, have a nice day," and he did.

(Woman)   I have post-partum depression. I do something wonderful – the best thing I think I have ever done – and it goes out the door and I know I will never be able to produce anything like it again, and as I fail to produce anything quite like it again I fear I will be exposed for the fraud that I am. This is my personal favorite depression and I own it and treasure it.

(Woman)   I have been accused of being neurotic. I am wondering if it is a good thing to be neurotic if you are an artist.

(Genn)   John Cleese reports that he is able to be most creatively zany just before he has his periodic check-ins at Broadmoor for a mental ironing out. Perhaps the neurotic mind knows a richer range of emotion, particularly feelings of anger and aggression. If Adolph Hitler had been a better artist perhaps he wouldn't have taken up dictating. Tales of neurosis among the artists are plentiful. Vincent of the missing ear, etc. Salvador Dali built a career around pretending to be crazy. It's enough to make you think you have to be.

I'm not sure. Many effective artists that I know seem remarkably sane. At times they make the regular folks look neurotic. I like the quote, "No man is sane who does not know how to be insane on the proper occasions." It's those "proper occasions" which are the operative words.

(*Man*)   Words that appeal to me in the key word list are business, frustration and taxation.

Business: I feel I must try to treat my art as more of a business, and pay the rent from it, and save for the future. I want to be more organized so that eventually I can build a studio. This will involve making more contacts and treating art more as a business than I do now.

Frustration: I must try to balance my personal joy with the need to paint for a market.

Taxation: I am confused and worried all the time about taxation. More and more of us borderline artists are being driven underground.

(*Genn*)   I think you should put your mind at ease and register and pay the tax. You want it to be fair, and this would be a good place to start. If everyone were to pay a little tax, then there would not be such a load on the industrious and highly successful ones, and those that would normally pay no taxes will have a feeling of participation. I see no point in exempting people at the bottom end. It rewards poor achievers.

(*Man*)   What about income tax for artists?

(*Genn*)   Income taxation penalizes workers and rewards non-workers. It is not so much a tax on income, it is a tax on work. If governments feel they must levy a tax on work, then they should perhaps tax prayer and joy and hugging and kissing and other useful things. This is why I rather like the idea of a sales tax, because it's a tax on consumption, and the worker who makes the income may or may not choose to be a consumer. With the way things are the revenuers are in a win/win situation.

My rationale on taxation is that I didn't become an artist to make money. That may sound hypocritical to some of you. I became an artist because painting gave me joy. There is life after taxes. Decisions to travel and learn, like business decisions, need not be tax-driven.

It's useful to note that artists and other self employed persons can take advantage of a wide range of deductions and depreciations. For example a boat (floating studio), aircraft (needed to go places and get inspired), motorhome (mobile studio), summer cottage (secondary studio), airline tickets, hotels, seminars, the list goes on. All of these are reasonable expenses for an artist. Many professions do not have the advantages that artists do.

(Man)   Do you split your income with your wife?

(Genn)   Yes. With the children as well. A Retirement Savings Plan is also useful.

Unfortunately, the preparation of income-tax returns has become a high art, and, like art, not everybody can afford the best. I would like taxation better if it were more of a science.

(Man)   Yes, but if you are making thirty thousand a year you do not have enough to pay your rent and buy your materials.

(Genn)   At thirty thousand a year you can make it into a zero income-tax situation. What I am trying to do in this seminar is to help you get into my miserable situation.

(Man)   Regarding the Canadian sales tax, if I am in a craft show and I make thirty-one thousand a year, tax will be a part of my pricing. But the person in the next booth is only making twenty-nine, and tax does not figure in his work. That's not fair.

(Genn)   I guess what I am trying to say to you is to shift from the position of having to worry about 29 to 31, and rather go for 100 or 200 or more. You will do that by letting someone else represent you. I think you should attract specialized people around you; essentially dealers who know what they are doing, so that you can be free to work at your craft.

This may sound a cruel thing to say, but the poorer your work, the more you have to think of angles. You must think of promotional stunts, become your own sales person in cold malls, and endure the ignominy of supermarket parking lots. Through all of this talk there is an underlying axiom: Nothing beats good work. What I see before me is a person with quality work, but who is underestimating his potential. The idea is to lift yourself into the next level. Have higher expectations.

I had a car accident in my Jaguar roadster this summer, and I broke three fingers in my left hand. I was more than a month in a cast. When I came out of the cast my hand was like a board. I could hardly move my fingers. I went to a physiotherapist who was a pleasant, small woman with hands like a logger. We worked together, and day by day we got my fingers moving again. They would go so far on a Thursday, and a little bit farther on Friday. There was pain involved. This is the same with our work. You get to a point where things are working, and you must push yourself further. You must refine, and enlarge, and put more into it. In the words of Emile Coue, "Every day, in every way, I'm getting better and better."

When you have made another turn in your progress, or reached a new plateau, don't have any fear about going back to a gallery that has turned you down. When the dealer says, "I have seen you before," tell him, "Yes, but you haven't seen this."

(Man)   Do you mean one agent who distributes to dealers, or just one dealer?

(Genn)   I mean dealers. Most dealers want to deal directly with the artist. They need your personality and your peculiarities as much as they need your work. They need anecdotes, stories of your travels, stories of your quest. Agents and middlemen are the second to last refuge of second-rate artists. The last refuge is a grant. Artists who make an art of their lives and buckle down and get good at their craft will have less trouble weaving a network and thriving.

(Man)   Some of those agents sell to corporations and private homes.

(Genn)   That's a different type of dealer. They are called consultants, and they perform a very useful function. I include several of them among my dealers. For some reason they are mostly women. They take paintings up and down in elevators for a commission. During recessions hardworking consultants seem to do steady business. I think it is because a lot of dealers get lazy in good times by lurking in the back of their shops waiting for people to come in. And when customers stop coming in, they don't know what to do.

I tried to understand the marketplace during recessionary times. I discovered that some folks remain better off than ever. Even during the Great Depression people were buying Packards and Pierce Arrows. It was more by luck than design but during the last recession I did the exact opposite to what most of my competitors were doing. They were making small economy paintings and trying to supply the suddenly poor. But the bottom end of the market virtually dried up. I made big expensive paintings during the recession, and that is indeed where the market turned out to be. Consultants helped me do it. A lot of boardrooms and wealthy homes acquired Genns during that period.

I know some of you are thinking that I am a crass commercial person who has sold out to Mammon. I'm always getting credit for being a good businessman. During the recession there didn't seem to be much happening, so I went to work and challenged myself with big complex paintings. One of my working axioms is to keep busy while waiting for something to happen.

(Woman)   Mr Genn, was it always easy for you?

(Genn)   When I was just starting as a painter, I was in an art gallery one day and there was an older, respected artist there whom I barely knew but whom I admired, and who I would have liked to know. I was enquiring of the dealer if any paintings of mine had sold, and he said there hadn't been anything, and I said, 'I wonder why?' This older respected artist said abruptly from across the room, 'Because they're the shits.'

It took me about ten years before I could tell that story. His unpleasant remark hardened my resolve. Truth motivates.

It is never easy for any of us, even if we are highly talented. When I was a teenager growing up in Victoria, I had a good friend in Fen Lansdowne. Fen had polio when he was younger and was disabled. He had dropped out of high school and was dedicated to painting birds. Even then his work was excellent. One day Fen and I got up some courage and drove down to the Provincial Museum to show his work to Frank Beebe, who was the official artist for the Museum. When Frank looked at Fen's work he recognized its quality, but he warned that Fen would never make a living out of it. Fen asked him what he should do with his life, and Frank thought for a while and suggested, 'Saw filing.' On the way home Fen stewed about the idea of putting a sign out and offering a filing service. The thought made him angry. When Fen got this way we used to call it 'bloody minded,' but it drove Fen even harder in his bird work. I think that was the day he really decided to go for it.

I learned from Fen that within ourselves we can do anything we put our mind to. Negative ideas can be fought back and conquered. As Louise Hay says in *You Can Heal Your Life,* "It's only an idea, and an idea can be changed."

(Woman) What do you think about associations such as the American Watercolour Society, the Federation of Canadian Artists, or the Royal Canadian Academy? Are they relevant in promoting yourself?

(Genn) In some countries association means a lot. In the U.S. if you receive the top award of the year as a watercolourist by the A.W.S., that can mean a lot to a career. Americans are quite democratic in that way. In Canada it doesn't make much difference whether a person is an R.C.A. or not. I think it is because Canadians are generally more individualistic, or maybe they have a contrary suspicion of group-thinking.

But groups such as the Federation of Canadian Artists have their value. Their seminars and workshops are often excellent, and the spinoff connections with professionals are valuable too. Socializing with interesting people is always fun. The F.C.A. will take anybody with forty dollars.

In the old days academies tended to be the traditional preserves of conventional wisdom, often becoming arbiters of taste. They have a history going back to Plato's academy. A literary academy, the Academie Francaise, founded by Richelieu in 1635, became a bastion of conservatism and excluded many great french writers including Moliere, Balzac and Flaubert. This example shows the nature of the beast. The British Royal Academy, the French Academie Royale des Beaux-Arts, a major Russian academy, the A.K.h.R.R., and recent avant garde academies, serve social, educational and often political needs, and tend again to be safe havens for the conventional wisdom, and sometimes mediocrity. They are pleasant places in which gregarious artists may feel comfortable. For better or worse, we've now entered the age of the individual.

(Woman) Referring to your key words, what do you mean by 'box canyons'?

(Genn) Box canyons are places in life and in art that you ride up into and find they don't go anywhere. Sometimes they are hard to get out of and you have to go back the way you came in.

(Woman) I would be interested in what you mean by 'orgasms.' That word is also in the list.

(Genn)   Some learned people think that paintings are sublimated orgasms, that creativity is sublimated sexuality. It would be valuable to study the sex lives of artists, but to my knowledge no one has yet got them to hold still long enough.

(Man)   Another key word. What has 'boxing' got to do with painting?

(Genn)   Prizefighters report swings that miss the mark use up more energy than swings that connect.

(Man)   What do you think of people who copy your style? You have a lot of admirers. Their work is in galleries. I used to be one of the ones who copied your work, but now I've gone on to other things.

(Genn)   I don't lose a lot of sleep over it. Some of them I have encouraged. I hope researchers in a hundred years will be able to figure it all out, and put first things first. Galleries with integrity don't exhibit clones. Many professional artists, especially those who have been at it for some time and have developed unique styles, are often complimented on some of their work with someone else's name on it.

(Woman)   Mr. Genn, you were a juror for an art show which I entered. What is your criterion for judging?

(Genn)   I look for good work, and I look out for bad work. Were you accepted by the jury?

(Woman)   No.

(Genn)   Curiously, most sponsoring bodies want jurors to find more 'ins' than are sometimes deserving.

(Woman)   You look at the names, don't you.

(Genn)   Never.

(Woman)   How come the same names always get in?

(Genn)   I guess the same names do better work.

(Woman)   Many people like my work.

(Genn)   I am sorry but I don't remember the occasion. There is generally more than one juror. Perhaps I was one who liked your work, but my vote was overruled.

Jurying is a difficult business because it is a great responsibility for the jurors and a threatening step for the entrant. I take jurying very seriously. Not all juries are run the same way. In my opinion shows that require jurying should be juried by other artists, preferably three or more, and of wide-ranging tendencies. All jurors should have the power of 'in' and any 'in' vote should have veto over any 'out.' 'Ins' can be in the form of an anonymous card laid beside the work. The number of works to be hung is determined by the number of cards down. In the event of a short slate the jury might be pressed to lower their standards. I have been a jurist dozens of times, and generally I'm asked to continue in my search for virtues. Jurying is best done with a secret ballot so that no juror with perceived seniority or strong personality can get control or influence the other jurors. I think discussion about the relative merit of works should be discouraged. A silent jury has integrity.

If prizes, honors or special mentions are to be given, the jury should start looking at entries with multiple 'ins' until they match up with the prize range. Perhaps other entries with lesser 'ins' should be considered until the slate is settled.

Very often artists require jurors to state why they were rejected, and a secretary is engaged to take notes for the benefit of the rejected artists. In my experience the same criticisms tend to be repeated by the jurors, often in unanimity. The commonest complaints are poor composition, uninteresting subject or rendering, too tight, poor drawing.

If you have an art club or an exhibiting group, you might try self-jurying. This is where everyone can vote for their ten best works, say, with the exception of their own. Names can be taped over if you wish. If you keep bringing new faces into the group, the unpleasant personalities will not be unjustly rejected.

(Woman) What do you think about celebrities like Red Skelton and Toller Cranston getting into the art field and taking advantage of their name to promote themselves?

(Genn) More joy. It's a fine activity for high profile folks to look into, so they get a further sense of accomplishment in their lives. If people buy the paintings, that's their business. If they hold a parade down Main Street for Tony Curtis, that's show business.

Winston Churchill was a rather good painter. He wrote a

charming little book called *Painting as a Pastime*. In it he says that when he dies and goes to heaven, he wants to spend the first million years painting, so he can get to the bottom of the subject.

Hour 8

Seven Secrets

(Genn)   Here's what I feel you need in order to become an effective artist. There are seven key ideas on a sheet which you have and I would like to go over them with you.

The seven ideas are: strategy, work, set, clock, alone, rejection, and distribution.

Strategy:

It is vital to plan where you are going. Plan your year, your month, your day, your hour. I don't believe in showing this plan to anybody. Keep it to yourself. Showing it lessens the need to carry it out. You can work out your plan by the hours you wish to work or by the accomplishments you want to achieve. Accomplishment to accomplishment is better than time to time, I think, because, if you are a procrastinator, you can always say you are getting somewhere when you are only filling in time. It takes a little self-understanding to know which is best for you.

Here's an example of strategy. Robert Bateman has a rest period every afternoon between one and two. He asks and gets the full cooperation of his family. During this sacred period he accepts no phone calls or visitors. After a short sleep he feels rested and renewed – in a way he gets two days for the price of one. It's part of his plan for getting the best out of himself.

Regarding sleep, recent studies using university students as subjects indicate that creativity is the first faculty to suffer with the lack of a good night's sleep.

Work:

See your work as the key to your personal happiness. It sounds as though I think a person should be totally oriented to work, and compulsive about it, but in my findings effective artists tend to be this way. In spite of all the other elements that come and go in your life there is still the strong foundation of your work. I like to call it the 'escape into productivity.' People who are fulfilled in their art see their personality through their work. And as you get on in your art, you will find also that others begin to see you through your work. You can be an insignificant little person, but it is your work that will be you. Perhaps this is a tangible result of the realization that 'art is long, life is short.' Humans decay, art goes on. When homes are on fire, people grab paintings and run out with them. Art is a permanent extension of personality.

Set:

It is a good idea to make sets and explore variations on themes. For example, you might give yourself a goal to explore everything about dahlias in an 8x10 format. You will get a sense of accomplishment, and ideas that you had early on will be superseded by richer developments later. On my first day at Art Center School the instructor asked us all to produce a lot of roughs relating to a single idea. The roughs were to be 2x3 inches. He wanted 300 of them, and he wanted them by noon. This seemed an impossible task at first, and by eleven o'clock when I had two hundred done I was running out of ideas. Then I looked over at a couple of classmates, and they were exploring in areas I hadn't even thought about. By the time twelve o'clock rolled around, I was just starting to get into the good stuff, and I realized I could go on for days. To see the work of the entire class was electrifying.

It is a big mistake to get precious about our paintings. Most of us are only on page three of a three-hundred page book. Making long sets can help release us from this hazard. Give yourself the opportunity to explore further ideas within a given, even microcosmic, area.

This year I have been working on my principle of microcosm. I pick a small area and try to explore it thoroughly. One project has been the Robert Louis Stevenson Trail in central France. I have done it twice this year. It is a 120-mile walk that Stevenson took in 1878 together with a donkey by the name of Modestine. From this trip he wrote *Travels with a Donkey in the Cevennes.* Along the way he did drawings of the country and the people. While it is still a remote area, it is now possible to do most of it by car. The countryside unfolds in the same way, the hotels are under the same name and often owned by the descendants of people Stevenson met. Ruined chateaux are a little more ruined, and pleasant brooks that he contemplated still wimple into the Loire. I repeated his drawings, and read his book under the chestnut trees he describes. I was able to connect with Stevenson across one hundred and twelve years and two European wars, and it helped me to realize just how permanent and beautiful some things are.

Clock:

Minutes, hours and days are ticking away on us. It took me a long time to come to terms with this one. Traditionally, I have gone for the serendipitous flow of work, and the joy that goes with it. But I found that many fulfilled artists are interested in the clock. They are able to work to the clock. Not just a vague concept of time, but of 'clock.' They understand *tempus fugit,* and how precious and short life is.

When I fall off the wagon, I put myself back with a wrist alarm which can be set to remind me when the hour turns over. I have painted in a little country village in Derbyshire in an old parsonage next to a church with a belfry tower. Every hour it gave me the time, and on the quarter hour as well. How wonderful to be thus regulated and measured by the sound of the passage of time.

In my studio I sometimes use an elapsed time meter, which is installed on the console beside me to keep track of easel-time. One day at a yard-sale I purchased an industrial punch-clock that went off with a bang when I put a card in it, but then I realized I was going too far.

Alone:

I think you need to act as if you are an island and no one can help you. Artists must come to terms with aloneness. When young art students come to my studio I ask them how they enjoy being alone. It isn't necessary to be an introvert, but artists must somehow be their own best friend. In aloneness they learn to extract the best from themselves.

With regard to an assistant in the studio, I think it is important that he or she not be an artist in the same sense as you are. The purpose of the assistant is to do the things you don't want to do. Art is seldom consultative.

You are alone. You are an island. No one can help you. Books are the exception. Books are your treasured friends, and you can access them in your own sweet time. You don't have to apologize to them when you put them down. With books you can push many ideas through your system. But it is important to keep the time spent with your books in balance with the production of your work. There are some artists, particularly those who would be on the cutting edge of the avant-garde, who are umbilically connected with the art media, and they suffer from an information glut. I know artists for whom the news is so exciting and voluminous that little of their own work gets done. Circumspect aloneness with books is what I would aim for.

With regard to aloneness I quite often hear of problems concerning a spouse. Interfering criticism or interfering enthusiasm can both hurt an artist. An unimpressed encourager should be kissed regularly.

Rejection:

It's the basic principle of the game. We dislike being rejected. There is often a kind of blindness when we paint, and it is possible to be unaware how terrible our work can sometimes be. People say they are just as good as Cezanne's, but they can't understand why the world isn't buying their apples.

It is necessary to put yourself out for rejection, and accept that you will be rejected. At one time I was submitting gags for magazines, and I collected a wall of rejection slips. Sometimes an editor would write, "This gag very funny," on my gag, but the old pink slip would still be in there. I came to enjoy my slips. I collected them. I prepared new fresh envelopes and when the gags came back they went straight into the new envelopes and back into the mail. It was great fun. But the monumental wall of rejection slips was sending me a message about my sense of humor. I wasn't as funny as I thought I was.

I realized that when somebody was rejecting one branch of my work, they were accepting some branch of someone else's, and when they reject someone else's, they will be accepting mine. The important thing is to get the work out and around so it can be rejected. I am willing to bet that I have been rejected more than everybody in this room.

Distribution:

Go for the hook-hours. This is an expression that fishermen

use. It means that if you have five lines in the water, with ten hooks on each, and you leave your lines in for ten hours, you will have 500 hook-hours. That's how professionals catch fish. Amateurs toss a line in here and there.

If you have your works on the right walls for the right length of time those works are going to be finding friends. They might even be snapped up. Certainly you will get nibbles. Like the fisherman, you will be making a connection.

(*Woman*) I loved your remarks about your field trips. When I travel and paint I get so excited I don't eat, and in my case that's good.

(*Genn*) The way to see the sunrise is to rise before the sun. A restaurant is not the place to be at sunset. Roloff Beny, the photographer who did *To Everything There Is a Season,* rested at midday so he could be on location for the day's two main events. He took his big meal at noon. For me hunger in the daylight hours is solved with nuts, raisins, sardines, hearts of palm. Sit-down dining is done after dark. As Peter Ewart says, "There is something to be said for going alone, you don't have to keep regular hours." To be alone with nature is to be one with nature. In order to find out about things you have to be on the yellow brick road when you can see.

(*Man*) Regarding making a connection, how do you deal with people who only want to borrow your things?

(*Genn*) I used to be very fussy and particular about that, and I seldom let out any freebees or loaners. Lately I have been more casual. There is a time to sell and a time to give, a time to lend and a time to lease. Some of the most charming stories about artists involve gifts and loans. A friend of mine has an A. Y. Jackson which he gave her after she saw his socks were holey and she knitted him a pair.

By renting paintings the artist gets a small income, but best of all he gets to keep the work in his own possession. He can draw on them for shows, or bring them back into the market at a higher price later on.

Leasing paintings is another area. This is where a doctor's office or company gradually own an artist's work by regular monthly payments. They are able to deduct it as a legitimate office expense along with the furniture.

If you take the price of a painting and multiply it by .0328 you will get the amount the customer should pay to amortize a work over thirty-six months. This sits well with the revenuers.

Price of painting(s).... $1200.00
Multiplier....   x   .0328
Monthly payment....   = $39.36

The actual amount (including interest) paid over thirty-six months will be $1416.96

This is called a "capital lease." At the end of the term the painting may be purchased for a nominal price which is below the fair market value at the time. This amount is generally set at 10% of the value of the painting at the beginning of the lease. The periodic lease payments are considered to be payments on a financed purchase, and the original price of the painting is capitalized and depreciated while the calculated interest is deducted as an expense over the term of the lease.

Another type of lease is called an "operating lease." This is a rental for a given period, at the end of which the painting may be purchased for the then fair market value. In this case the periodic lease payments may be deducted as an expense and the purchase price paid at the end of the lease is capitalized and depreciated as office furnishings.

These two are examples of 'correct' procedure. I have seen a wide variety of custom deals, some in which the artist is paid out in three installments and in less than one year. These seem to work with the revenuers, too.

(Woman)   You emphasize habits as a key to everything. What do you mean by habits and how do you achieve them?

(Genn)   The wise bag-lady in *The Dreamway* said, "Habits are more holy than messiahs." She was talking about those good habits that make life workable. Certainly artists who have good habits save themselves a lot of trouble. We *are* our habits. Bad habits tyrannize us though a lifetime of error. Bad habits are learned and can be unlearned. I think brand new good habits can be had at any stage in our lives.

When I was in grade two I brought home a report card that said 'Bobby has lazy habits.' I don't know how I got all of those bad habits, but I know my mom picked up after me too much. In grade three I made up my mind to overcome my laziness. I'm still working on it. I still know I'm basically lazy, I just don't act lazy anymore.

It's essentially a matter or realizing the head-body relationship. The head, on top of the body, directs the body. The body does what the head says. Head does the thinking. It thinks that the body needs to do this or that, so it tells body and body does it.

Now that you've had that advanced lesson in motor function, I'm going to show you how to conquer your bad habits. I think you can change just about anything if you have the will. Start with something modest – something in which you know you can succeed. Work on that one small area for a given time. Let's say you have the bad habit of a messy palette. Make a project out of it and give it a week. Tidy up and reorganize your palette area definitively. Work out an entirely new system if you see a need, say by putting your colours in a definite order. Now, conscientiously and consistently keep them that way. At the end of the week you can assess the exercise, and give yourself a longer time period. Once you've gained confidence that you can master small bad habits, you can move on to bigger bad habits such as lack of concentration or procrastination or impatience.

I'd like to draw your attention to a popular book. It has seven more good things in it. It is called *The Seven Habits of Highly Effective People,* by Stephen R. Covey. Here are his seven habits and what they mean:

1. Be proactive.

To be proactive means that as human beings we are responsible for our own lives. Our behavior should be a function of our decisions, not our conditions. We have the initiative and the responsibility to make things happen.

2. Begin with the end in mind.

The habit here is to start with an image or a picture as the frame of reference of where you want to go. This means planning your hours and days and even your entire lifetime. It is important to avoid busyness for busyness' sake and to keep goals foremost.

3. Put first things first.

After you have become opportunity-minded, as opposed to problem-minded, you set your mind-power into action to set priorities. You place urgencies ahead of non-urgencies, and turn the pages of your personal book in a clear and thoughtful order.

4. Think win/win.

Win/win is one of the six paradigms of human interaction. It is a frame of mind that constantly seeks mutual benefit in all relations. All parties feel good about the decisions and feel committed to the action plan.

5. Seek first to understand, then to be understood.

This habit requires a shift into genuine empathy. Most people do not listen with the intent to understand; they listen with the intent to reply. The idea is to get inside the other person's frame of reference.

6. Synergize.

Synergy means that the whole is greater than the sum of its parts. When channeled the parts are catalytic, empowering and unifying. With synergy you start on an electrifying adventure, because you can't know the outcome.

7. Sharpen the saw.

This habit means expressing in balance all four of our principal motivations, the physical, mental, emotional and spiritual. It makes the others possible, and puts them to work.

Now before you dismiss Mr. Covey's ideas as too woo-woo for your pragmatic nature, I would like to say that when I looked at his material I related it to the trials that artists go through. So much of the self-pity, lack of joy, and lack of progress I have noticed in artists is not brought about by lack of ability, but by an undealt-with lack of character. To put it simply, in order to produce art we need to learn the right habits.

(Woman)   What is art?

(Genn)   Perhaps it's the proper confluence of heart and brains and courage through the medium of an acquired skill.

St Thomas Aquinas thought it had to do with beauty. He thought beauty involved what he called *Integritas, Consonantia,* and

Claritas. His first step was to put a frame around something and look at it as a subject worthy of contemplation while isolating it from everything else (Integritas). The next step is the craft – arranging everything inside the frame so that it is in harmony (Consonantia). When harmony has been attained – one achieves radiance (Claritas). The work stands on its own as a thing for delighted contemplation in itself, and does not need explanatory notes.

There are other possibilities. Let me give you a couple of examples:

One day I purchased 5,000 plastic pill-bottles with lids. It took a station wagon to get them to the studio. Over a period of months I put different 'things' into the bottles: nuts, bolts, shells, grains, pebbles, toys, feathers, bones, sticks, shards, dirt, mechanical parts, dingbats, beautiful things, unspeakable things. I engaged friends to help with the project. Kids by the schoolfull were pressed into service. Bags of bottles were taken on trips and filled up.

I had big display cases made for the bottles and stood them around the studio. One day a dentist friend of mine who was looking them over said, "Why is it that when an artist does something like this it's called 'art', but if someone like me did it, it would be called 'stuff'?"

Here's another attempt to identify what art might be:

A friend of mine who is a creative and sensitive guy liberated an enormous illuminated sign from a Home Oil station in the days when we still had Home Oil. With some effort he was able to set it up in his living room. I remember sitting there with Dave sharing a bottle of wine in the glow of that great word 'Home' and agreeing with him that it definitely was 'art.'

I am sure you can see by these two examples that one's point of view is a factor. Mine has changed during the time I've been painting. As the sentiments of art are widespread and often commonplace, I tend now to feature and honour craftsmanship in my appraisal of art. I also look for cleverness. I love clever ideas, inventive new uses of media, clever handling of old subjects. Art is what you want it to be.

"Art is what you can get away with."
Marshall McLuhan

"Art is long, life is short, judgement difficult, opportunity transient."
J.W. von Goethe

"Art is long, life is short, unless your medium is jello, then art is short, life is long."
Anonymous

"Art, being quite useless, except to the soul, is the highest of all human endeavors."
Bruce M. Rogers

"'I don't know anything about art, but I know what I like,' really means, 'I don't know anything about art, but I like what I know.'"
Anonymous, corrupted from
Max Beerbohm

"Art is unthinkable without risk and spiritual self sacrifice."
Boris Pasternak

"Art! Who comprehends her? With whom can one consult concerning this great goddess?"
Ludwig van Beethoven

While it's fascinating to find out what everyone thinks art is, perhaps it's a matter of choosing what you love to do and giving courage to your hands to honour that love.

A recommended book is *The Courage to Create,* by Rollo May. He suggests that creative people of whatever stripe have a natural and powerful human instinct that is difficult to extinguish.

A friend of mine took me up in a hot-air balloon over the Alberta foothills. It was a sunny winter day with a magnificent and threatening chinook arch over the Rockies. As we lifted off I contemplated that my companion was over seventy and I was not sure I would have been able to control the balloon if anything happened to him. I panicked and sat down on the floor of the gondola for a while. There are no seatbelts in a balloon. It's just a creaky wicker basket which you could step over into thin air. From time to time my companion fired up the burners. We drifted silently along, suspended in space, and, looking down, I could see our tiny shadow moving slowly over the snow fields of a magic land far below. Gaining confidence, I set up my easel, squeezed out my paints, and made the best part of a 12x16.

I will never forget the look on the faces of a couple of men who flew close by in a Cessna. At 6,000 feet they saw somebody who was doing 'art.'

(Woman)   Do you think that words can help a person to be an artist?

(Genn)   Let me give you an answer that has to do with words. In this segment we seem to be working with sevens. Here is a little story which has seven parts you might find helpful.

One evening I was invited to do a demonstration of an acrylic painting for a woman's art club. I didn't know any of them, and when I arrived and was setting up my easel, I realized I didn't have any white in my paint box. For a few minutes I contemplated the idea of trying to do the demo without using white. I told them my predicament and asked if anyone had any white to lend me. The answer was no, they had come to watch and learn.

I had to think of something, so I asked if I could do anything I wanted with them. I told them that I would do something new to help them become better artists. They seemed to want to cooperate. So I hypnotized them.

Anger and skepticism came over some of their faces as I asked them to lie back in their chairs and give me their minds. Some would not assume an open position and sat there with their arms folded and glared at me. Others closed their eyes and blissfully let me do my thing. I had never tried this with a group before, but I knew that Reveen, the well known hypnotist, could do it with a full theater, and that a percentage of them would be receptive and open to suggestion.

Going through the standard procedure I saw that some of the women appeared to become rather relaxed.

I spoke as Reveen-like as I could, and put in as many quotations as I was able to muster so it would take up more of the allotted time. I suggested seven directions for the women to take. Here they are:

1. You will have a rebirth in your seeing. You will now be independent of the expectations of others, and you will have a fresh new vision of the world. Simple things will come alive for you.

2. You will begin to concentrate on your art for a set time every day. You will now awaken each day with a desire to find out what the day will bring. You will work like a robot and you will not tire from it.

3. You will be guided by your intuition to seek those areas in which you need to improve and which you have been avoiding. You will enrich yourself with new areas of study and you will develop facilities previously unknown to yourself.

4. You will take joy in building on those areas which you now do well. You will put your assets into regular practice and experience an increase in confidence and self-esteem. You will see the flower of your personal style grow before you.

5. You will beef up your volume. You will paint so much that you will pass through amateur noodling and into professional bravura. You will put your bad work behind you through sheer production.

6. You will now overflow with personal confidence in the knowledge that you are in full control of your artistic destiny and that with the deep resources of your subconscious mind you can accomplish anything you want.

7. Like the turning on of a light you will gain a brilliant new satisfaction in the work itself. You will bring to it a degree of completeness, and you will take pride in it and both expect and find fulfillment and success when you show your work to others.

Then I brought them back to life in the usual fashion. Some had been only listening. Others, surprisingly, took a while to come around. Several left for home immediately. One woman rushed up to me and put her arms around my neck and said, "I don't know what you said, but I have the feeling that this was the most wonderful thing that ever happened to me." Some were all aglow and wanted to stay and talk. One woman said she had come to learn something and instead she got 'this.' I gathered my things and left. One woman phoned the studio every day for a month to keep me informed of her progress. I've never been invited to do a demo for that group again.

Hour 9

Adding Value

(Genn) I want to give you one idea that will pay for the whole seminar. It is such a golden idea that I would appreciate it if it didn't go any further than this room.

I keep four words foremost in my mind when I'm painting. The words are; *Put More Into It.* I call it *P.M.I.I.,* and I have a sign on the studio wall to remind me.

What this means is, without cluttering the painting, I ask myself how can I put more into it, how can I give it more 'points.'

To illustrate what I mean I'm going to give you a standard example – some of you will say a campy example. Let's say we have a snow scene which is well enough designed and painted. Give it an arbitrary three points. If we put the moon in the painting, we might give it another point. Providing the moon is integrated well it will perhaps make the work more fulfilling. Now let's put a small cabin in the painting, and give it another point. Turn a light on in the window of the cabin, for another point. Now let's tie a horse to the cabin. Another point. Let's put a young woman in the window. Perhaps the woman in the window was going too far, and will merit the deduction of a point. Taste is all-important.

I think you understand what I mean. Other elements can be points too. Design can merit points, as can style, colour or condition.

Ask yourself, 'What is the condition in this painting?' The condition could be wind, or rain, or sunlight, or moonlight, or season. Think of the names of some of the great paintings by the Group of Seven: *'The West Wind', 'Spring Break-up', 'Northern River.'* The title gives you a clue to its spirit.

When we think this way, we give 'value added' to our efforts.

What I am suggesting is that you push yourself into better, richer, more important work. Give it a sizzle and some magic.

Now there are people who think this concept of value added is the very height of crass commercialism. I feel it adds more joy, fun, and excitement to your life as an artist, and therefore to your work. There is more connection and more exposure of personality when you put this idea to work.

Here's a further idea. This year I have been twice to the Rousillon in the south of France. The vine-covered hills around the farmhouse where I stayed are lined with cart tracks, and beside these tracks I found the remains of ancient grape-carts, many of them more than a hundred years old. They would have broken down in the fields at harvest time and been pushed off to the side to moulder into the landscape. As I painted these relics I noticed that all of them had a zinc or copper plate screwed to the whippletree, near the front of the cart. I started carrying a screwdriver around with me, and I unscrewed these plates and brought them home.

The plates are generally small and oval, and carry the name of the man who was the controller of an appellation. A plate might say: *'Joseph Jorda, Proprietaire a Estagel, Py-Or. Canton de Latour de France.'* Estagel is the name of the village where M. Jorda operates. Py-Or means Pyrenees Orientale, and the canton is the municipality.

When it comes time to send the painting to a dealer I include the plate with the delivery. The dealer can then phone a special client and tell him he has something special to show. If he wishes the dealer can fasten the plate to the frame under the painting. Or he can just include it as a gift to the buyer when he sells the painting.

Here's another idea. Sometimes I feel literary and I write a little story or an anecdote that took place around the making of the painting. I take the material and put it in an envelope and tuck it behind the stretcher. This offers another connection, and years after I have forgotten what I wrote, people are still taking them out of the envelopes every few years and reading and remembering what I had to say.

Here's another idea: When I go on sketching trips I take accurate maps with me and later make photo-copies of significant areas, and I put an 'x' with a coloured jiffy-marker at the places where paintings were generated. In Ireland, in a remote corner of Donegal, I did a painting called "Grace O'Flaherty's Driveway", and I included such a map with the painting when it went out of my studio. Recently a letter arrived from a Montreal collector who said he had made a special and laborious trip to the exact spot to see the place for himself. "You didn't quite get the right green," he wrote.

These ideas are nothing fancy. They don't cost a lot, but they make a connection between the artist and the collector.

Recently I've been doing paintings of various French villages. One of my favorites is the remote hill village of Montaillou, which is near Ax-les-Thermes in the southern part of the country. I wouldn't have found Montaillou if it were not for the book of that name. I have had to order extra copies of the book so that it can be given with the paintings.

Let me tell you about the book. In the middle ages the village of Montaillou had a great many Cathars, a type of heretic. A zealous Catholic inquisitor was dispatched to clean up the village, and over a period of five years he interrogated virtually the whole population of some four hundred souls. Accurate notes amounting to many volumes were taken, and the result was a few unfortunates burning at the stake and the cutting out of the tongues of a few liars.

In 1979 these old records were released by the Vatican Library, and the French author Le Roy Ladurie assembled the inquisitor's material. Ladurie has produced the most intimate and fascinating insight into the sociology of a village of the Middle Ages. Traditions, attitudes, superstitions, agricultural methods, home life, sex life, are revealed in stunning detail. In a time when there were no wheels in this village, no glass in the windows, little in the form of money, we come to know common folk, clerics, and titled persons as though they were characters in a novel. These people were incredibly dirty; social life often centered around de-lousing. Strict codes of behavior existed in the community, and those codes were forever being broken. A lot of fornication went on in Montaillou. For some reason most of it took place on the dung heaps.

After I had read the book I went to the village and sat on the very spots I had read about. Farmers, the descendents of the characters in the book, stooped in the fields to gather turnips, and eyed me with suspicion. Shepherd boys and girls stood among their flocks in the twilight. I wandered in the church, climbed through the ruins of the chateau, and carefully inspected the dung-heaps.

The experience of Montaillou has been for me what Bernard

Berenson called 'life enhancing.' It has been an opportunity to connect with people and broaden their horizons as well as mine. The book is called Montaillou, and it's by Emmanuel Le Roy Ladurie. It's available in English.

(*Woman*)   I would like to share something which I learned from one of my teachers. He had determined that there are six elements you need to make a successful painting. These are:

Movement: Try to have something moving in a painting, the wind, waves or other form of motion.

Life: There should be some form of life in it, human or animal. Or evidence of the hand of man.

Light and dark: Good work has a strong sense of contrast and a full range of tones.

Strong source of light: It's important to have a single and determined source of light.

Marriage of colour: Establish a tonality and integrate the colour in a harmonious way. This is an equivalent to the concept of mother colour which was mentioned earlier.

Indentions and protrusions: Areas should either recede or come forward, generally effected with warm and cool colours or with darks and lights.

(*Genn*)   Excellent ideas all. Your list reminds me of five elements which I often think about when I am at work. Here they are:

1. Gradation in a large area.

2. Strong pattern.

3. Warm against cool.

4. Grey to rest the eye.

5. Colour surprise.

You can demonstrate the value of these five elements with a simple abstract sketch.

I have said several times that nothing beats quality work. The painting makes a connection and 'sells' when you paint it, not as is popularly believed, when it leaves a gallery. One of the most important factors is the quality of the composition.

Books have been written on the subject. Here are some suggestions to add to your idea bank:

Break with conventional wisdom. Traditional ideas, such as the golden mean, balance and unequal breakup of areas can be examined and played with. For example, figures generally look into the picture area, such as in the painting Whistler did of his mother. Try a composition in which the figure looks out of the picture area, and note the effect. Pictorial stress will be set up and a larger composition taking place beyond the edges will be defined.

Eye control. Take control of the observer's eye. Lead him in, show him where, circulate him around your work. Composition through eye control is a subtle way of holding interest in your work. If you don't hold the viewer's attention in this way you will have to do it in another.

Patterning. Successful compositions often have strong patterning, either in tone value or colour. Additional interest and variety is created with the repetition of commonplace motifs such as stripes, blocks and spots. Gerard Manley Hopkins wrote:

Glory be to God for dappled things-
For skies of couple-colour as a brinded cow;
For rose-moles all in stipple upon trout that swim.

Colour composition. Pay attention to the mother colour – one hue that is dominant throughout the work. Sophisticate your greys. Choose surprise colours with care by cruising your palettte and asking "what if." Know when your colour composition is monochromatic or analogous or complementary.

Format thinking. The proportions of the format require different compositional approaches. Be aware that a 24" x 36" dimension requires a different plan than a 24" x 30".

Good composition knows its edges. When you do a sketch, draw the format first so you can find out how the pattern fits.

Long horizontal formats generally require long horizontal subjects or opposing tensions. A tall vertical format often requires a strong verticality. I like Robert Frost's remark when he was asked why he wrote within the confines of iambic pentameter: "I think I play better tennis because the court is there."

An excellent exercise as well as a viable method for building compositions is the 'place & solve' system. In this the artist commits himself to one element, say a figure in the foreground. Degree of commitment will be related to how finished he wants to make it at the time. Then he asks himself what shape or shapes he needs beside or behind the shape already established. Let this shape suggest something – a car, a tree, a lion. Now the work begins to take on meaning as well as composition. Keep going. What other interesting shapes does it need, and what do these suggest? Patterns and motifs that remain essentially abstract will add magic and mystery to the work.

(Man)   Years ago Charles Scott of the Vancouver School of Art used to tell his students that a 'value plan' was important. A painting must work in black and white and all the intermediate tones, before it can work in colour.

Yesterday we were asking why seven million women didn't become prominent artists. And we were talking about how it's hard to get away from the conditioning that keeps women at home ironing and baking pies. I would like to say that there are a lot of men who have similar problems: cutting the grass, planting the garden, holding down a job. It made me think that there might have been seven million men whose names didn't show on the list because they were too worn out to even think about becoming artists.

Becoming an artist won't happen for some of us because we have a fear of success, or a fear of failure, or perhaps guilt. I worry that art may destroy my relationship. I don't know how those around me would react if I got into art in a big way.

Charles Scott said if your value plan is right, then your painting should work. If art is not working for you, perhaps it is your value plan that isn't right. You could substitute for value plan, your belief system.

(Genn)   Robert Bly, in *Iron John*, which should be required reading for all men, and for mothers of sons, talks handsomely about male mentoring and male initiation, and where our values and belief systems come from. By tracing the myth of the wild man and the search for the key which the myth says is hidden under the pillow of the mother – and must be stolen by the son – we get a glimpse of our potential and god-like strength. A lot of men are afraid to free up the wild man within.

(Man)   Rejection was one of your key words. When I grew up I became a real-estate developer. As you know everyone dislikes real-estate developers. At public hearings I was vilified for bulldozing trees and ruining the environment. I know about rejection.

Now that I am an artist it doesn't bother me to be rejected. If someone thinks my work is poor it is not a factor, because I am now strong and I have enjoyed doing the work.

Regarding what Robert has said about our potential, I think that most of us here should have realistic expectations of where we are able to take ourselves. I feel that art and talent and success are related to an instinct to flourish.

(Genn)   I'm coming from the belief system that anyone can flourish if they put the best of their mind to it. And flourishing for me has meant the adoption of what I call good habits and continuing to push myself when the trip became depressing.

When I was growing up in Victoria, there was a sampler on my bedroom wall. It showed a little boy lying in bed with the sun streaming in the window. The caption, stitched there by my grandmother, was, 'Many are called, but few get up.'

I feel we must give ourselves permission at any stage in our lives to take the power and seize the day.

With regard to understanding our limitations and our capabilities, I'd like to quote Sir Philip Sidney: "If you shoot at the mid-day sun, you can be sure that you will never hit the mark; yet you will be sure to shoot higher than if you aim at a bush."

(Woman)   Picasso was quoted as saying that when he was a child his mother used to ask him when he went to bed at night whether he deserved to sleep. In order to deserve sleep he must have either learned something or accomplished something on that day. He was still doing this in his nineties.

(Woman)   Picasso was a very self-centered and egotistical person. How important do you think ego is?

(Genn)   Very important. In the Andes in Peru a few years ago I met a reclusive artist. I was attracted by his work, and when I came to know him I was struck by his personality. In the course of a day's conversation he repeatedly implied three things about himself.

1. I know exactly what I am doing, and I do it very well.

2. There is no one in the world who is doing anything really important right now, except me.

3. Today's works by me are tomorrow's treasures for all the world.

This egotistical fellow went by the name of 'Cosmo.' He came originally from Decatur, Illinois. Alone, high in the Andes, he could foster his fantasy. Every day in that rarified atmosphere and critic-free environment gave him further proof of his genius.

Cosmo made me realize something. Many artists whom I admire have, in some degree, his basic beliefs, and they try to enact the qualities they imply.

1. *Pride.*   He or she adopts an individualist methodology and has excellence of execution.

2. *Importance.*   He or she has the feeling that it is worthwhile to pursue his or her own direction.

3. *Value.*   He or she has a sense of place in history.

These attitudes are voiced at gallery openings, in studios, in classrooms, in cafes, and in humble garrets. They may appear boorish and rigid but they are the secret notions of many artists. Sometimes one hears genuine humility too.

(Woman) All these qualities are not worth anything unless the artist is noticed.

(Genn)   To want to be noticed is a natural human drive. The condition is not equally present in all persons, but most would like to be noticed at certain times and are willing to pay a price to receive that notice. Clothing, automobiles and offspring are typical opportunities for notice open to all of us.

As the peacock spreads and struts its tail display, so the creative person flaunts his talents, whatever they may be. In a field of peacocks of equal display, the effect is diluted by the number of competitors. The higher animals have the advantage of a greater range of individuality and sublimation of expression. A unique effect has more chance of being noticed.

Seen in the context of basic needs, the schools and trends in the history of art take on a new perspective. The formation and espousal of meaningful new trends are an attempt to fulfil this basic need to gain attention, and may not be taken as seriously as the observer might assume.

Such egocentricity, whatever impels it, has traditionally been seen to have a higher incidence in artists, and when added to talent, capability, craftsmanship, or dogged hard work, can lead to flourishing success and personal satisfaction.

When an artist feels his work is going nowhere, to no venue, and is generally ignored, he may feel there is no point in continuing. A talent, as they say, should not be hidden under a bushel, and a person may opt for another life path, perhaps with other expectations. Furthermore, when the available talent in an individual is low, then the recourse to differentness is a very real option.

(Woman)   What you are saying is that an artist should create a mystique around himself.

(Genn)   Not exactly. I like George Bernard Shaw's remark that "You will think less of the art, when you know the artist."

The best idea is to let your light shine forth from your work, and forget about your image. The work itself is a reliable measure. Your efforts either communicate something to someone or they do not.

The artist's audience should have a general picture of where the artist is coming from. But I don't think it is a good idea to let people know too much. Further, it has been my observation that when an artist becomes too much of a publicity hound, success, even though it may be deserved, may be hampered. Publicity should be handled with care, not only regarding what is said, but in what frequency. Anything reported should be natural, understandable, and if possible, understated. Artists who trumpet their successes telegram a lack of self-esteem. Rock stars can operate on this level, but it is not always becoming of artists.

Being an artist is a delicate business at the best of times. I think you should make every effort to protect what you are. It's your life, your livelihood, and the source of your happiness.

(Woman)   What sort of publicity do you think an artist should seek?

(Genn)   Many artists actively look for opportunities to get publicity when they feel they need or deserve it. Some artists want it

when they simply dine out or have their hair done. Personality is news. Furthermore, the business of the news is often to find things that are 'new.' Not all art is news, some of the best art isn't new and never will be. Realistic and even avant-garde art is frequently passed over by the media.

If you want publicity, it is useful to try to establish some newsworthy event or occurrence that goes along with the work, one that will suggest or imply the quality of the work, without actually saying so. Watch out for the secondary implications that go along with the news, and try to get a little control over what you give out. Here are a few somewhat extreme examples which will illustrate the effect of secondary implication.

News Item	Secondary Implications
Artist mauled by bear while painting.	Artist takes chances while working in wilds. He is a dedicated artist.
Artist burns paintings rather than pay big taxes.	Artist is mainly in it for the money. He is masochistic.
Artist has big success.	Artists don't all starve. Artist must be good. Artist must have 'sold out' to commercialism.
Artist starves to death in garret.	Artist was dedicated (re-enforces starving artist myth).
Artist paints giant work.	Artist is 'big'. Artist is show-off.

Some artists feel that any publicity is good publicity as long as the media gets the name right. I had a young grizzly watch me paint once, but I didn't feel it would be worth my while to get her annoyed.

(Woman)   Don't you think artists need publicity to survive?

(Genn)   Not as much as you're probably thinking. I have found it is effective to allow people to discover you, one at a time, in a gentle, unhyped, and thoughtful way.

The subject of this hour has been to discover ways that we can add value to our work. As usual we have wandered, and the wandering has been fun. I would like to sum up with a few specifics on the adding of value:

1. Add personality.

Put your personality to work in your paintings. Don't do what you think someone would like. Give the viewers a piece of your soul. Let them see your joys, your desires, your unique perspective.

2. Add importance.

Try to break through the mundane and ordinary. Great artists take ordinary subjects and monumentalize them. Take the time to construct works that subtly offer more than the average.

3. Add size.

Good ideas that have been tested in smaller works gain power and authority when enlarged. This does not mean you have to paint big for the sake of bigness. Add size when the subject asks you.

4. Add mystery.

Paintings without mystery are too easily processed by the mind of the viewer. Elements in a work can be partly hidden or in a state of emergence. Invite participation by allowing the observer to complete areas himself.

5. Add quality.

Cruise the work carefully and honestly as it nears completion. If a hand or a face has given trouble, it might be necessary to scrape off and go back in. The sight of your stroking should give joy to yourself and therefore to others.

I know this might sound basic to some of you, but I want to mention five physical items for your studio which will contribute to added value in your work.

1. A professional easel. You need one that will stand up to you when you push.

2. A proper easel chair. It should be hard, armless, with a springback, like an old secretary chair.

3. A well lit workstation. It should be of consistent colour temperature, as shadowless as possible, and dimmable.

4. A sturdy palette table. Efficient for time and motion, correct for your handedness.

5. A secondary easel and an easy chair. An artist needs a cocoon in which to contemplate his moves.

Your studio can be a properly organized extension of your home. You move and arrange the elements of the studio to suit yourself. When it is right and proper all things are possible in it. Robert Louis Stevenson wrote:

What are you able to build with your blocks?
Castles and palaces, temples and docks.
Rain may keep raining, and others go roam,
But I can be happy and building at home.

(Man)   With regard to your value added concept, I would like to say a few things. I feel you can only add value if your work represents and communicates the conscience and truth of the times we live in. These times are often ugly and threatening. I used to be weak and mousey. Right now, as many of you know, I am doing characters who scream and whose bodies melt away into raw meat. My paintings roar and rage at people. To me these works are icons of our age and have value.

(Woman)   Regarding those screamers that you are painting, what if people don't understand what it is you are trying to say?

(Man)   Only about ten percent of people relate to my work. But that's okay. I don't care about the others. It is something that I do. If it pleases me that is all that matters.

(Genn)   You're a lion, not a mouse.

(Woman)   Mr Genn, do you believe in trying all kinds of mediums and art forms?

(Genn)   As Richard Bach said: "Learning is finding out what you already know. Doing is demonstrating that you know it." I like to try everything to find out what I am not good at. I've tried pottery and ceramics a few times and it's not for me. I started a bowl once and it ended up a small conical affair so I decided it was a salt shaker. I got the little holes in the top all right, but it wasn't hollow. I rationalized that my salt shaker would be exellent for persons who were trying to cut back on the intake of salt.

Hour 10

Gathering Up

This is the part where we gather up the loose ends and take a look at concerns we might have missed. Is there anything you ever wanted to know but were afraid to ask?

(Woman) I want to know more about photography. How much of a tool is it for you?

(Genn) It's a most valuable tool. If Leonardo da Vinci had been given a Kodak he would have valued it. He would also have found that it is a treasured servant and a dangerous master.

The camera was used as a studio tool by such artists as Corot, Delacroix, Vuillard, Sickert and Degas. The happenstance crop and edgemanship that Edgar Degas achieved was largely due to his use of the camera viewfinder. A book called *The Artist as Photographer,* by Marina Vaizey, covers the uses that artists of today and yesterday have made of the medium.

These days the collecting of candid material on location is most effectively done with the 35mm. format. I call it 'stealing' because the artist doesn't usually gain permission to obtain these images. In country markets, or anyplace where people go about their business, the camera is indispensable. Distracting backgrounds, telephone wires, and the like are not such a problem as they are to photographer's who would aim for quality photographs. An artist may get material at random knowing that he will later 'mix and match' his images.

A typical photo opportunity for me is the annual Indian ceremonials in Gallup, New Mexico. The subjects are all around you, they literally flood the viewfinder. I have found that 'before the parade' is an ideal time. At this time your subjects wait for you. They are used to being photographed then and are at ease with photographers, which is the way one wishes them to be. In crowds where people are less likely to enjoy being photographed such as in Arab countries, I have at times used a right-angled mirror in front of the camera lens. With this device you can look one way and take the photo in another.

It is a good idea when shooting in subject-rich environments to get shots of potential props and peripheral material. These become important later as you assemble your reference for your paintings, and they enrich your idea bank.

When I'm cruising for subject matter to put into my camera, I watch out for what I call 'alpine meadows.' This is more of a feeling than a place. You get out of the car and you just know you're not in Kansas anymore. I started using the term when I was a teenager. I was at Paradise on Mt. Ranier for the first time, and was impressed with the perfection of design, the spacing of elements, the ready-made beauty and magic of the place. But this experience might come in a village in Portugal, or in watching people moving in a reflection on Japanese paddies. The point is to recognize it as a 'hot spot' and overshoot. It's impossible to have too much reference material of a subject that moves you.

It is also useful to gather elements that can later be assembled into a whole. The foreground, for example, is a vital part of a land-scape. Get it right and the rest tends to take care of itself. Sometimes I put myself into 'foreground thinking,' and consciously winnow foregrounds out of otherwise uninspiring areas.

Controlled posing of a portrait subject in a studio or on location requires thought and planning. I like to have two or three cameras loaded and ready. I think out all of the locations and positions as generously as possible so that I will shoot more material than I need. I move the model or models around quickly, sometimes physically, shooting all the time, keeping one eye on the face and one on the hands.

In indoor situations, natural light from a window is best. I often have my assistant hold a photoflood close to the shadow side to give a warm counter light and to fill in the shadows. I sometimes augment with a bounce-flash. Strong cast shadows from the brows, nose and lips are to be avoided. The modeling of the face and cheeks is all important. I like to get a fairly strong core-area somewhere on the face. A sharp bright light at some distance at eye level gives a sparkle to the eyes if necessary. I use a fairly fast film and sometimes overexpose a stop or two in order to burn out in the light areas and allow me to see detail in the shadows. My shoots are quick and painless.

I make separate colour notes of the eyes under several different light conditions. Film does not always get it right.

A medium focal length lens (55 to 70mm.) is best for portraits in order to keep from putting too much weight on the model. To avoid pincushioning or unwanted distortion care should be taken not to get the face too close to the corners of the viewfinder, particularly with wide-angle lenses. There are times when wide-angle lenses of 25 to 35mm. can be used effectively to achieve 'leggy' looks and other interesting distortions. Also, you can distort and transform things to your liking when you refer to your photographs later.

I currently use a Canon E.O.S. 650 with a 35 to 135mm zoom, a lens that handles most situations. Autofocus and autowind, which I swore I would never use, have turned out to be unbelievably handy.

I carry a camera practically all the time. I find it helps to heighten my visual awareness, and there are always those times when it is necessary to save a fleeting situation.

A valuable side issue in photography is using a photocopier for paste up and compositional planning. Images can be put together and copied, repeated, enlarged, reduced, squeezed, elongated and distorted with the use of this machine. Compositions can be planned and worked out quickly in the studio. It is possible to work with photographic prints, drawings and thumbnail sketches, or a combination of all.

(Woman) Does Fen Lansdowne, the bird painter, work from photographs?

(Genn) He assimilates what he needs for a given species from a variety of sources. From museums he borrows birdskins, then he adds his knowledge from books, the photographs and paintings of others, and his considerable observation abilities in the outdoors. He has an uncanny ability in drawing, and an accurate sense of colour. I have never seen him use a camera.

(Woman) Does Robert Bateman, the wildlife artist, work from photographs?

(Genn) Photographs lie around Bateman's easel. Artists of this genre rely on the medium. They are in the business of showing

us and honouring the creatures which share our fragile planet. Wildlife artits need to get it right – to supplement their knowledge of movement and musculature observed in the field.

Just a few decades ago the eminent painter Carl Rungius used to shoot the moose and then prop it up as best he could in a lifelike position. John James Audubon was an excellent shot. The likes of Bateman and Audubon use different shooting instruments.

(Woman)   Do you have a specific plan when you go out to get material with your camera?

(Genn)   I try to open my mind to all subjects, even if I'm looking for just one thing at the time. If I'm looking for rocks, I also shoot for the day I will need clouds or trees or barns.

Some artists don't like the idea of using a 'bag of tricks' as a tool in their art. They prefer the free flow of intuition or association in order to discover direction or style. I think a balance of the two methods is of value. The idea is to add to your innate creativity a private checklist which represents your best mental effort when prepared in a quiet and reflective time.

I notice when heading out with my cameras to get material my mind is often flooded with ideas – but when confronted with the actual subject and new surroundings my creativity somehow dwindles. Here is the first part of a list that I use for portrait shoots:

1.   subject is distant, thoughtful
2.   decentralized pull in composition
3.   the props of subject's profession
4.   unusual angle or unusual light source
5.   hands in or hands on some object
6.   syntagma
7.   height of feeling or action
8.   subject and object eye line up
9.   screens, veils, sheets, masks
10. busy detail interest
11. telephoto pile up
12. wide angle distortion
13. high or low vantage
14. silhouette and subject
15. get inside action

16. cut with edge light
17. planned patterning in design details
18. dull subject, smart angle
19. smart subject, dull angle
20. mystery and fusion

(*Woman*)   What is syntagma?

(*Genn*)   It's a motion-picture term. One subject dissolves into another and establishes a new relationship. Syntagmas are everywhere and they can add interest to your work. An example would be a sunny face and the sun.

(*Woman*)   You have a lot of lists. Where do you get them?

(*Genn*)   I make them up. Here's how. I note down what I think I do differently and what is important to me. Then I try to determine what I am doing right. I look for elements of style and try to define them in my own way. I ask 'What could be?' Then I search the literature and the admired work of others for further items and I invite them to become mine. I now allow the two sources to cross-pollinate one another and enrich my list.

(*Woman*)   How do you get all your ideas?

(*Genn*)   I get them when the idea valve is open. I save the ideas with notebooks, sketchbooks, and tape recorders. The idea valve is more likely to be open at certain times.

At bedtime: The body is relaxed, the brain is pillowed, and there are no pressing physical needs. Ideas come from reading or events, and bubble up from the subconscious or as fantasy. When ideas come thick and fast, I call it 'pop, pop, pop'. Ideas must be put down *ad hoc* in the full knowledge that they will be reviewed later in a more circumspect light.

While driving a car: The cerebellum is busy guiding and controlling the vehicle, while the engine and running gear hum along. The landscape winds by, presenting a series of images, relationships, words on signs, which cross-fertilize with current thoughts. 'Pop, pop, pop.'

While boating or fishing: Boats contrive to bring ideas up from Davy Jones' locker. I have a theory that the brain's beta-wave is leveled out by floating on water and by the dominant horizontality of the setting. Fish interfere with the process. The Irish writer Oliver Gogarty used to fish without a hook on his line so he could dream.

Towards the completion of a painting: I get ideas as the work nears its end. Satisfaction or disappointment trigger the 'pop, pop, pop' – new ideas come out of old ones.

During conversation: The company of stimulating people adds new frames of reference. I like language. With it I discover ideas I didn't know I had.

For the most frequent manifestation of idea time, I have four words:

Alone.	(space to contemplate)
Free.	(no pressing responsibilities)
Inspired.	(recently seen excellence)
Triggered.	(passing material at hand)

(Woman) You mentioned that you prefer slides to prints. Could you talk a bit more about that?

(Genn) I think slides are the best reference medium. Here's my reasoning:

1.   They are infinitely enlargable and reducible.
2.   They have more than enough detail.
3.   They are less expensive than prints.
4.   They are printable, projectable, and they can be viewed on a microfilm monitor.
5.   They are easy to archive in slide sheets, and are relatively permanent and colour fast if stored correctly.
6.   The image is reversible when projected, which increases the versatility of the reference.
7.   They are defocusable when projected, which is an asset in proving up a composition and locating compositional faults.
8.   They are distortable by projecting from an angle.
9.   They are traceable without fuss.

Some artists seem to have trouble seeing projected slides in very bright studios. I have a dimmer for my studio lights on the console beside my easel. I use a standard Kodak Carousel with several wide and narrow projection lenses for various applications.

(Woman)   What about working outdoors?

(Genn)   Some artists find outdoor work natural. Strangely, these artists may do poorly when trying to synthesize in the studio. Others never get the hang of outdoor work and don't care for it.

I believe it takes a certain type of personality to master painting outdoors. The word 'simple' comes to mind, although this is not always true. The mind should be a settled one, used to and capable of a kind of patience in tranquility. This artist often feels an affinity for and a positive attitude toward the outdoor act of art. It was said that John Constable sat so still while painting outdoors that a field mouse once crawled into his pocket.

A little time spent in setting up is useful. I try to make sure that what I have chosen is right for me at the moment. There is nothing worse than getting started on something and then discovering that there is something better nearby. I like to decide whether the job will be 'direct,' that is, a ready-made scene or subject, or an 'assemblage,' a re-composition or transformation. I watch out for unpleasant line-ups such as trees coming out of people's heads. I study areas that may cause trouble and try to think of how I will approach them. I move trees around. I agree with James McNeil Whistler when he said, "Nature is usually wrong."

There are artists who simply take the subject as they find it. Very often these artists just feel a painting coming on, and this feeling determines where they will stop and go to work.

A concern for outdoor artists is that God works with light, while painters work with pigments. Transposing light-ranges into palette-ranges becomes the main job. If the relative lights and shadows are right then half the work is done.

(Woman)   You seem to wander here and there for your outdoor work. Do you let the subjects 'find you'? You mentioned serendipity a couple of times.

(Genn)   I was on one of the Aaran Islands off the west coast of Ireland. It was the slow season and several carts and their horses waited silently in the misty rain outside the only pub on the island. Business was obviously poor so I reasoned I might get a cart for a day for a small figure. I entered the pub, identified the drivers, and ordered a half Guinness. I asked if any one of them would care to give me a 'serendipitous' tour for the day. One of the drivers, Seamus McFinn, didn't catch my meaning, but he was willing to take me out.

I told him I was an artist, and I just wanted to take a look around and paint a bit. I told him I didn't know what I wanted till I saw it, and I promised him it wouldn't be much work for the horse.

He told me the horse's name was Jack, and that Jack would appreciate an easy day, so we made a deal.

Before I could finish my drink we were on our way, wrapped in blankets, grinding and lurching down a misty roadway. About ten minutes out I saw something I liked. Seamus let me set up in the cart. He walked around, smoking his pipe, and chatting with passers by, most of whom seemed to be relations of his. Sometimes he would drop by the cart and say something like, "See his honor over there, killed an Orangeman once, he's my cousin, he's a mean one."

During the day we moved from place to place, never very far. Once we passed a small building by the side of the road and I asked him what went on in there. He told me it was a factory for leprechaun parts.

During that lovely wandering day I got a good start on three small paintings. Toward evening the sun came out and it was time to go back to the pub. Seamus hadn't said a word about my work, he didn't seem to care. As I was putting my stuff away he looked at one of my efforts and said, "And that will be serendipity, never heard of it. C'mon Jack."

(Woman)   I read an article in which you said what is necessary to be an artist is to have 'an iron will, and a butterfly mind.' I feel I am doing pretty well in the butterfly mind department. It's the iron will that evades me. You imply some sort of old-fashioned self-regulation. How do you do this?

(Genn)   You have to write your own regulations. You know yourself better than anyone, and you can target your problem areas. You also need the ideas of others. Stephen Vizinczey wrote a piece called *The Writer's Ten Commandments*. This is the sort of thing I mean; I think you could change 'write' to 'paint'.

1.   Thou shalt not drink, smoke or take drugs.
2.   Thou shalt not have expensive habits.
3.   Thou shalt dream and write and dream and rewrite.
4.   Thou shalt not be vain.
5.   Thou shalt not be modest.
6.   Thou shalt think continually of those who are truly great.
7.   Thou shalt not let a day pass without rereading something great.

8. Thou shalt not worship London/New York/Paris.
9. Thou shalt write to please thyself.
10. Thou shalt be hard to please.

(Woman) In your list of 'key words' you mention 'album.' Is this where you store your slides?

(Genn) I meant an album where you keep photos of your work. Your album can be a modest book or it can be an extensive archive. Its purpose is to order, date, and anchor your productivity. It is a pleasant form of bookkeeping. It chronicles your loves and enthusiasms. It gives pride to the stream of your production, and is a destination in itself. You can set yourself to work for your album. If it's a fancy place, it can be a worthy destination.

There are, however, dangers in albuming. By laying your work out in ready accessibility you may lock into a style, rather than thinking each new work out on its own. The idea of preciousness in your work is well worth guarding against. There is the likelihood that you will keep track of your winners and repeat them. Even worse is the possibility that you will keep track of your losers. Bad work can haunt you, jinxing your current work, and pull down your spirit. The job of an artist is to move away from what he considers his failures.

Do you notice how I am always saying there are two main kinds of this and that? Did you know that there are two main kinds of people? One kind feels that there are two main kinds of everything, and one does not. I am of the former kind. I think there are two main kinds of albums.

1. The serendipitous album.

There's that word again. This album suits the jumpy mind and the creative spirit. It includes only the high points, and functions only when the albuming muse is upon you. It includes interesting and essential work, period changes and breakthroughs. It is for the stuff that is really worth keeping and that you can't live without. There is some satisfaction in knowing that even though a work has been sold, it is still yours to have and to hold through your album.

2. The comprehensive album.

This album suits the more orderly mind, the accumulative type, the collector. It is also for the artist with a sense of his place in art history. This album attempts to include everything. It is a record of historical progress for the benefit of the artist and those who come after. How lovely it would be to have a record of Mozart's or Velasquez's linear progress.

There is an ongoing debate as to whether prints or slides are the best medium. Prints do seem to be handier, and they album well. Polaroids are the choice of those who would have instant gratification. I prefer slides for reference, prints for finished works in my albums. Prints, at the present time, transfer better to photocopy and fax. Slides are the accepted medium for submission to galleries. Electronic albuming, with its speedy indexing and retrieval, is now just becoming practical for artists. Further to photocopy, I like to have a photocopy backup of good stuff that my assistant can take home in case of a fire in my studio. Colour for this purpose is still expensive. Black and white does the job.

I think it is a good idea to separate clippings of achievements, awards, articles, notices, and advertisements from the general album activity. I'm not sure, but I don't think it's a good idea to mix up what others think with my personal journey.

(Man)   How many paintings in a year would you paint, and how many would you sell?

(Genn)   I paint between two and four hundred. Size influences volume. Also, when I work on my printmaking my original work is less. I couldn't give you a figure on what sells, but it would be lower than total production, as my inventory is slowly building.

(Man)   Do you keep a personal client list of people who buy your work?

(Genn)   No. Galleries do that.

(Woman)   Have you kept an accurate personal record of everything you have done?

(Genn)   No. I wish I had. About 1974 I started a system, and everything since then has been documented. My assistant set me up with a simple card file. Each card shows one painting, its title, size, when it was painted, and the galleries it has visited. When it is reported sold, it goes into a sold file. Thus we are able to identify works when they come onto the secondary market. Sometimes col-

lectors write and ask for more information about the works they have, and with the card file I am able to pinpoint periods and trips for them. It also comes in handy when I have to show the revenuers that I have been where I said I was.

(*Man*)   Do you trust your galleries that they will sell your paintings for the price you put on them?

(*Genn*)   I suppose there has been some profiteering here and there of which I am not aware. Some artists send spies to check on prices. I trust the people I deal with. They are sweethearts. If there were a problem, I'm sure it would come down the grapevine.

(*Man*)   When you send paintings out on consignment, the dealers sometimes wait six months before they pay you.

(*Genn*)   True. But they eventually pay because they want more paintings. Practically without exception all the people who handle my work are straightshooters. Most dealers treat artists with respect.

(*Woman*)   What makes an ideal dealer?

(*Genn*)   Honesty, enthusiasm, loyalty – also love of art, love of people – those are some characteristics I look for. But there's more to it than that. Being an effective art dealer is also and art – and some have a talent for it and others do not. It's a sort of intangible thing – the closest I can come to it to say that the best ones have a quality something like *empathy*. Good art dealers are not always sharp salesmen in the traditional sense – some of them are not even particularly good businesspeople. But they do know how to listen and they do know how to be quiet at the appropriate time.

A dealer who says something like "those colours would go well in any room," is setting himself up for disappointment. Sincerity and truth are all important. That's why silence is so golden.

In an art gallery the work of art speaks quietly for itself and to the customer. It enters his or her perception through the emotions, recollections, feelings, ideals. It starts to connect. The dealer can be instrumental in bringing the customer to this point, or in reinforcing after the fact and building interest by *sharing the excitement* – by telling well what he knows about the artist or the circumstances under which the work was produced.

My most effective dealers often make good friends with their customers. They keep them posted as to what their artists are doing. They know and care about the passions of both their artists and their collectors.

There are several tendencies among dealers.

1. To be a picture shop. This dealer hangs stuff on his wall and sees if anybody wants it.

2. To be a discriminating gallery. This dealer uses his own taste or an education as a guide. He is often passionate, erudite, and in the vanguard.

3. To be in perennial serial exhibition. This dealer, through constant one man shows, offers a new flavor every week.

4. To be a sharer of magic. This dealer is an informed go-between to the artists and collectors he can work with, and enriches both.

Many successful dealers show some of all these tendencies. Unless asked, I try not to make recommendations to help them in their business. They all have their own way and it works for them. Some dealers find it disagreeable when they discover that their artists are better businessmen than they are. Some dealers are brilliant.

Just before a show and prior to the public's arrival a clever dealer allows a few minutes to let the artist explain the present work to the gallery staff. This candid information, specific location, anecdotes, or sometimes humorous insights, which only the artist can give, are valuable to gallery people in creating interest and connection in the work.

I like dealers who are interested in historical art, who pay attention to the secondary market and support and trade in the previously sold work of the artists they represent. I like dealers who help people build collections and add fun to the confidence. Good dealers have books behind their heads.

Dealers with the art of dealing in their bones may wish to simply let the intuition flow – others may see that dealing is a specialized form of retail sales where systems such as the *Friedman Method of Retail Selling* can be used to enhance the pleasure and success of their business. I've observed that about ten percent of the dealers do ninety percent of the business, and location is not always a factor.

Artists do well when they use a bit of common sense in selecting or being selected by a dealer.

(Woman)   How do you know when you have gained acceptance?

(Genn)   Artists always wonder when acceptance will come. Professional artists tell of hesitant growth, with two steps forward, one step back. Artists in candid moments report of nagging fears of position and ability. They also speak of a tenuous snowball effect in their careers, a gradual building, a gradual affirming. American abstract artist Mark Rothko was so shocked by acceptance when it finally arrived that he produced one great last statement – a pool of suicidal blood.

Critic Herbert Muschamp reports, "it is exhausting to listen to artists go on and on about not getting their due – it's been a major hazard of restaurant life in lower Manhattan for years."

Andy Warhol, once he achieved centre stage, clung to this position with soul-destroying tenacity. Finally, media manipulation became his principal art.

The question to ask is from where you want your acceptance to come. Here are a few suggestions:

1. Acceptance by peers and competitors.

The community of artists is a noble house. Appreciation by fellow travellers is satisfying and fulfilling. Artists who work to this end have a chance of becoming artists' artists, and know better where they stand in the scheme of things.

2. Acceptance by critics.

Critical acceptance can make you a household word in some households, or it can spoil your joy. Catering to critics is poisonous to the soul, hazardous to the vision, and historically ridiculous. There is only one critic worth working for, and that is yourself.

3. Acceptance by the public.

'Popular' is a 'no-no' with most critics. They tend to represent the public as tasteless sheep, upwardly mobile, the type of folks who want to look good, be smart, and "with it." They are wealth-flaunters, and, worst of all, investors. I want to tell you a secret. The public is lovely.

4. Acceptance by target-groups.

These are the people with whom you wish to connect with and those most likely to relate to your enthusiasms. They can be ecologists, conservationists, gays, indiginous peoples, ethnics, women, angries, aficionados of sports, cars, aircraft, wildlife, etc. There is a pluriverse of possibilities.

(Woman)   What value do you see in attending the exhibitions of other artists, and could you comment on how commercial exhibitions work?

(Genn)   Attending exhibitions is part of the learning process. I recommend seeing public gallery exhibitions in two visits. The first round should be undertaken without information and alone. When you go by yourself there is no obligation to linger longer than necessary and to keep up with the pull or drag of another person's interests. During this first round you edit the work and form your ideas. A good system is to 'speed through and be attracted by,' to try to catch the joy, wonder and meaning of what you are seeing. At the same time try to see the overall effect as you would read the table of contents in a book. If the work has content or craft, you will find it engaging.

After you have established your own reactions to the works and if you feel it deserves further attention it is a good idea to return armed with as much information as possible. The guide-book, the tape, or the informed guide or companion enrich the experience when weighed against the initial feelings of the first round.

Just as some people go to movies to enjoy the filmic technique and pay little attention to the story, so artists often study the 'how' of exhibitions. The two-stage system of seeing allows an artist to be 'swept up' by the work, as well as providing directional and technical depth.

Openings at commercial galleries are informative of human nature. Often customers will line up outside so that they can get the best of the show. The first few minutes are important. I've noticed that successful shows have lots of action, with cross-gallery movement, talk, energy, and a sense of rummage-sale urgency. For the artist it's mainly a matter of standing around for a couple of hours and meeting old and new friends. My mother gave me the best advice when I nervously arrived at my first one-man show: "Be yourself."

Many shows are now cool and casual and there is time and the atmosphere for the people who attend to contemplate the work. In my mind these sorts of shows are the more desirable.

Every gallery owner or director has his or her own method of running shows, and I don't like to interfere. Some believe in pre-sales, some do not. Galleries and artists sometimes have to pay dearly through invitations and advertising to get the first red stickers to go up, and I believe in helping to pay for this. Generally the artist and the dealer share this expense 50/50.

(Woman)   I wonder if galleries are gradually becoming redundant. I'm on the internet.

(Genn)   The internet as a marketing tool for works of art hasn't quite happened yet – and it probably won't until private vehicles go fully into gridlock. Art, in order to be loved, should *be with* people.

Cyberspace is yet another space in which creative people may work. What it lacks in permanence it makes up for in reach. Right now the web and the internet seem to be best at conveying information and ideas.

(Man)   Do you serial number your paintings?

(Genn)   No. Numbers bother me. I know my work by title. Titles are the bridge between the artist and the viewer. They can arouse his interest and help him to understand the work. They can also annoy and aggravate him. I find there are five main types of titles.

Sentimental
Numerical
Factual
Abstract
Mysterious

Let me give you an example of what I mean. Say you had a painting of Mt. St. Helens in the process of erupting. Here are some of the titles which you might choose:

Sentimental: 'God's Wrath, The crack of Doom.' People actually put titles like that on their paintings.

Numerical: 'Number 16.' This title implies that the artist has painted at least 16 paintings of the subject, perhaps following the progress of the mountain from quiescence to explosion. It suggests seriousness and set.

Factual: 'Mt. St. Helens, May 18, 1980.' This is a no-nonsense title. It confirms the viewers positive identification of the mountain and the event. It satisfies and is pure by its lack of bamboozlement.

Abstract: 'Washington Pattern, Grey.' This title uses the formal values of the painting itself, by-passing the significance of the subject or event. It suggests another value to the subject, perhaps an artistic quality that sets the viewers' sensitivities into action.

Mysterious: 'Bill Smith's Dilemma.' Where is Bill Smith? He isn't even in the painting. Who is Bill Smith? What fearful thing happened to Bill Smith that day?

I think factual and abstract are generally the best titles. I believe in avoiding titles with a 'cutsey-pie' flavor. One painting I saw was of a pretty woman in a negligee, sitting on a bed looking wistfully out a window, while a cowboy was pulling on his boots. The title was *'A Hell of a Way to Make a Living.'*

This will be a good place to end our seminar. Perhaps you have the idea that this business of being an artist is a hell of a fun way to make a living. It's more than that. With your mind, your heart, and your courage, you give joy to your hands. If it were easy, everyone would be doing it.

Here's where I like to put a name to our seminar and what we have just done. Let's call this one *'The Painter's Keys.'*

(Woman) I think it should be called *'The Artist's Ruby Slippers.'*

(Genn) Thank you for attending. I sincerely hope you have gathered some new ideas from the exercise. You are a spirited group. Good luck to you all.

Appendix

(Handed to participants at beginning of seminar)

PAINTING

It is simply a matter of putting the right colour in the right place.

Equal intensity laybys
The big blur
Defocus
Warm against cool
Ajacent areas accepting temperature
Reflected light
Contrapuntal over-emphasis
Reinforcement of negative areas
Held and lost edges
Gradations
Sophisticated greys
Colour surprise
Coming to light
Activation
Strong value composition
Interpatterning
Local colour conceptualizing
The real see
The joyous stroke
Talk back
Flats
Tie ins
Pink focus
Avoidance of knowns

Key Ideas

Strategy- Plan your work; work your plan

Work- See your work as the key to your personal happiness

Set- Make sets, explore variations on themes, sizes, colours, mediums

Clock- Minutes, hours, days, ticking away

Alone- You are an island – no one can help you

Rejection- It's the basic principle of the game

Distribution- Go for the hook hours

Key Words

Acceptance	Emotions	Melancholy	Seeing
Activation	Empathy	Mentors	Self-pity
Adjacent	Entertainment	Metabolism	Selling
Album	Evolution	Mind	Senility
Alone	Exercise	Mirror	Sentimentality
Amateur	Expert	Modernism	Serendipity
Androgeny	Exhibitions	Money	Set
Anger	Exposure	Monotony	Shipping
Art	Facility	Mood	Shock
Atmosphere	Failure	Morgue	Shows
Avoidance	Fame	Motivation	Sickness
Beauty	Family	Mystique	Signature
Bicameralism	Finishing	Narcissism	Simultaneity
Biorhythms	Framing	Nature	Slides
Books	Frustration	Neatness	Socializing
Boredom	Game	Neurosis	Spirituality
Box Canyons	Gift	New	Starting
Boxing	Grace	Observation	Stimulants
Brushwork	Grants	Order	Stopping
Burning	Graphics	Orgasms	Story
Business	Guilt	Originality	Strategy
Camp	Habits	Outdoors	Studio
Career	Health	Paint	Style
Change	Hobbies	Palette	Success
Challenge	Honour	Pattern	Symbols
Cleverness	Humility	Photography	Synchronicity
Cliches	Ideas	Physical	Synergy
Clock	Impatience	Picturesque	Talent
Clubs	Improvisation	Plan	Taxation
Colour	Incentive	Planner	Teachers
Comparison	Influence	Play	Teaching
Commissions	Inspiration	Points	Technique
Competitions	Intimidation	Prints	Temperament
Composition	Inventing	Procrastination	Thoughtfulness
Condition	Inventory	Professional	Time
Consignment	Inverting	Progress	Titling
Contracts	Jealousy	Projectors	Togetherness
Copying	Jinxed	Public Galleries	Tracing
Creativity	Junk	Publicity	Trends
Criticism	Landscape	Quality	Truth
Culture	Leasing	Realism	Ugliness
Dealers	Libraries	Reaping	Variety
Depression	Light	Rejection	Will
Desire	Loneliness	Repetition	Women
Disability	Loving	Reproductions	Wonder
Distraction	Luck	Reputation	Work
Distribution	Madness	Resources	Xenophobia
Drought	Masochism	Risk	Yes
Economics	Masterpiece	Scheduling	
Ego	Materials	Schools	

Name Index

Idea Index

Painter's Keys Books

You can order further copies of this book directly from the publisher. Books are sent postpaid to anywhere:

USA: 14.00 USD
Canada: 16.00 CAD
UK: 10.00 GBP
Euro: 15.00 EUR

Please send check or money order to
Studio Beckett Publications,
12711 Beckett Rd.,
Surrey, BC., Canada V4A 2W9

You can also order this book on-line using our secure electronic payment at www.painterskeys.com/purchase/

Volume orders discounted for Workshoppers and Good Deed Doers on request.
Telephone: (Canada) 604 538 9197.
E-mail: rgenn@saraphina.com

Subscribe free to the
Robert Genn Twice Weekly Letter
and connect with a world-wide community of artists.
It's Robert's world-wide gift that artists love to get.
The letter and the website updates and adds
further valuable tips and information.

To find out about it please go to
www.painterskeys.com